"Melding concepts from a broad clinical practice with scientific updates and compelling anecdotes, this candidly written guide leads its reader through the complexities of alcohol addiction. Perhaps the most unique feature of this writing, however, is the authors' abilities to interweave ideas of compassion and spirituality into the matrix of this intricate disease. They demonstrate that faith is not incompatible with science—but complimentary!"

—DR. ROBERT MORSE, *Emeritus Professor of Psychiatry, Mayo Clinic and Mayo Medical School*

"Alcoholism doesn't run in my family—it flows through it. I wish I had known about *Dying for a Drink* thirty years ago when my father was battling his monster. This book makes so much sense and helps me understand my father, myself, and my family in ways that I might never had without it."

—JOEL LEE, *Associate Vice Chancellor of Communications, Vanderbilt University Medical Center*

"Reaches out and grabs you . . . should be read by every person concerned with alcoholism or chemical dependency."

—HAROLD E. HUGHES, *Former U.S. Senator*

"As definitive as anything I have ever read on the subject of alcoholism."

—RICHARD C. HALVERSON, *Former Chaplain, U.S. Senate*

"Undoubtedly the best book on alcoholism from a faith-based perspective I have ever read."

—ARCHIBALD D. HART, Ph.D., *Professor of Psychology and Former Dean of the Graduate School of Psychology, Fuller Theological Seminary*

DYING FOR a DRINK

DYING FOR a DRINK

Anderson Spickard Jr., MD
Barbara R. Thompson

W PUBLISHING GROUP
A Division of Thomas Nelson Publishers
Since 1798

www.wpublishinggroup.com

Published by W Publishing Group, a Division of Thomas Nelson, Inc., P.O. Box 141000, Nashville, Tennessee 37214.

W Publishing Group books may be purchased in bulk for educational, business, fundraising, or sales promotional use. For information, please e-mail SpecialMarkets@ThomasNelson.com.

Library of Congress Cataloging-in-Publication Data

Spickard, Anderson, 1931-
    Dying for a drink / by Anderson Spickard, Jr., and Barbara R. Thompson.
      p. cm.
    Includes bibliographical references and index.
    ISBN 0-8499-0847-7
    1. Alcoholism—Treatment. 2. Alcoholics—Rehabilitation.
  I. Thompson, Barbara R. II. Title.
    [DNLM: 1. Alcoholism—rehabilitation. 2. Family Therapy—methods.
    WM 274 S275d 2005]
    RC565.S67 2005
    616.86'106—dc22

2005022145

Printed in the United States of America

05 06 07 08 09 RRD 9 8 7 6 5 4 3 2 1

To

Caroline, Kate, Mark, Emily, Anna, Lucas, William,
Ben, Scott, Megan and Claire

and

Daniel, David, Kiera, Peter, Julia and Claire

Contents

~

Contents

Acknowledgments

~

In the writing of this book, and in our collaboration of more than thirty years, we have become indebted to far more colleagues, friends, and family members than space permits us to name. We are also indebted to numerous recovering alcoholics and their families for generously sharing their stories with us. Their names and identifying details have been changed to conceal their identities, but their records of triumph over adversity are true.

We acknowledge our debt to the many colleagues of Anderson Spickard, including Billie Alexander Avery, Josh Billings, Greg Dixon, David Dodd, Peter Martin, and Bill Swiggart for their professional assistance and faithful friendship. We are especially indebted to Diana Phillips for her calm, generous, and capable administrative support of our project.

We are grateful to our mutual and dear friends who have supported this project along the way. These include Howell and Madeline Adams, Sister Patty Caraher, Alfred and Carney Farris, Connie and Dale Nash, Myo Naing and Htwe Htwe, and the many friends of the International Community School in Decatur, Georgia.

We would like to thank David Moberg at Thomas Nelson for his

Acknowledgments

visionary support of this project, as well as Kate Etue and Adria Haley for their editorial assistance. A special thank-you goes to our proofreader, Suzie Jacobs.

Finally, we wish to thank our families, particularly Sue Spickard, Susan and Ron Gray, Anderson and Margaret Spickard, David and Alice Spickard, Burnett and Ramona Thompson, Brenda Cabrera, and Burnett Thompson III for their loyal support over many years.

ANDERSON SPICKARD JR., MD
BARBARA R. THOMPSON

Introduction

⌒

It wasn't a promising beginning. When I first started treating
addicted drinkers more than forty years ago, I believed, like many
doctors, that alcoholism was a hopeless condition that afflicted weak-
willed people. I did my best to avoid alcoholics in my practice, and
those I couldn't avoid, I rushed through the standard hospital treatment: detox, medical care for serious physical problems, and discharge through what was sure to be a revolving door.

My only "success" was getting rid of Henry, an old fraternity
brother. The more Henry drank, the more he presumed on our
friendship. He telephoned day and night, pressured me for pills,
and asked to be admitted to the hospital for imaginary illnesses.
Finally Henry called one afternoon, threatening, as he had before,
to jump off Nashville's new Memorial Bridge unless I renewed his
prescription for Valium. "Go ahead," I told him. "You're a pain in
the neck, and if you let me know the time, I'll invite our mutual
friends." I didn't believe Henry's threat, and I hung up on him
without a trace of bad conscience. I had too many patients who
wanted to get better; why waste time on a man, even a friend, who
was destroying himself? (Fortunately, Henry did not follow my

thoughtless advice and later entered an alcohol recovery program. He was sober for twenty-five years before his death from causes unrelated to alcoholism.)

GOOD INTENTIONS, A TRAGIC OUTCOME

In the early 1970s I went through a profound spiritual conversion that left me feeling more empathy for my addicted patients, which by now included three doctors. I felt that if God could help me, God could rescue them from addiction. I tried everything possible to help this steady stream of bright, gifted alcoholics find a spiritual solution for their addiction. I even handed out copies of the song "He's Got the Whole World in His Hands." Despite my good intentions, I never cured or even controlled a single drinking problem. I could only stand and watch as patients exhausted the last energies of their talented lives in pursuit of "just one more drink."

Then there was Jerry. Jerry was a tough, successful businessman, and our friendship went back many years. I knew Jerry was a heavy drinker, but by the time his frightened (and embarrassed) family brought him to my office, I had trouble believing the results of my own examination. Jerry's liver was barely functioning, and his pancreas was acutely inflamed. In the presence of his wife and children, I warned him that he would die in a matter of months if he didn't stop drinking.

Jerry was visibly shaken and vowed never to take another drink. His family supported him in his promise, and I was convinced Jerry would recover. Then, for more than a year, I watched in unbelieving sorrow as my brilliant, strong-willed friend drank himself to death. It was one of the most distressing experiences of my medical career. Never again would I dismiss alcoholism as a disease of weak-willed persons.

A LIFE-CHANGING ENCOUNTER

Shortly after Jerry's death, I went to a weeklong workshop at a pioneering alcoholism rehab center in Minnesota. My initial skepticism (What could I learn that I hadn't already heard in medical school?) turned to amazement as I watched skilled counselors lead groups of alcoholics through a comprehensive recovery program. Many of the counselors were themselves recovering alcoholics who had been sober for ten, twenty, and even thirty years.

Even now, I can feel the mix of astonishment and regret as I digested this new information. I was a professor at a major medical university, teaching students the most up-to-date medical science and unsuccessfully treating a large number of alcoholics. All of these patients, as far as I could tell, were drinking themselves to death, and neither I nor my medical colleagues knew of any reliable or medically sound alternative to benign neglect. I had tried to fill this vacuum by talking with my alcoholic patients about their spiritual lives, but even the few who recognized their problem were unable to give up drinking.

Now, after twenty years of medical practice, I was learning that alcoholism responded to a specific treatment program and that there were *recovering* addicts the world over. It was as if I had spent years ineffectively treating diabetic patients with prayer and good intentions only to discover that millions were doing quite well by controlling their sugar intake and using insulin. It was, to say the least, a rude and life-changing awakening.

A TREATABLE DISORDER

The field of addiction medicine has changed considerably since that time. Although the average medical doctor still fails to diagnose addiction *more than 50 percent of the time* (or to make an appropriate treatment referral), our understanding of alcoholism, its impact on families, and the tools for recovery continue to improve. Now, more than ever, alcoholism is a treatable disorder. All over the world, alcoholics whose lives have been devastated by their addictive drinking are finding healing for their bodies, minds, emotions, spirits, and relationships. Equally important, their families and friends are being empowered to begin their own recovery process.

My own involvement with alcoholics and their circle of loved ones has become one of the most hopeful and inspiring aspects of my medical practice. While setbacks are unavoidable, the joy of being a partner in an alcoholic's recovery far outweighs any disappointments. In the past twenty years this journey has taken me to communities around the United States and in the former Soviet Union, where one in three deaths are alcohol related. Through translations of the first printing of *Dying for a Drink* more than twenty years ago, my circle of concern has expanded to include recovery groups in countries as diverse as Korea, France, and Mongolia.

The success of *Dying for a Drink* rests in large part on the interviewing skills and compelling writing of my friend and colleague Barbara Thompson. I met Barbara many years ago when she was working with Ugandan refugees, and her concern for victims of war has endured to the present day. She is a co-founder of the International Community School, a groundbreaking school for refugee and mainstream children in Decatur, Georgia. I am grateful that she was able to take time from her duties there to write the revision of *Dying for a Drink*.

This updated version of *Dying for a Drink* has been produced to equip our readers with the information, tools, and confidence they need to participate in the recovery process. In the chapters ahead we will ask ourselves important questions, and we must be prepared to change long-standing opinions. For example:

- Who is at risk for alcoholism? Is there an alcoholism gene?

- How do you convince an addicted drinker to get help? What kind of program is best?

- How can family members and friends begin their own recovery process?

- What if an alcoholic never stops drinking?

- What about our personal drinking habits? What factors should govern our decisions?

In my forty years of medical practice, few experiences have had the resurrection quality equal to that of watching alcoholics and their families leave behind the living death of addiction. Today, while virtually every corner of the globe suffers from the debilitating consequences of alcoholism, the good news is that millions of adults and teenagers have found sobriety. It is my hope that this book will enable you and your loved ones to become partners in this healing journey.

ANDERSON SPICKARD JR., MD

1

An Equal Opportunity
Epidemic

~

James leans against a telephone pole in a liquor-store parking lot, drinking a forty-ounce bottle of beer. On the sidewalk, five teenagers do a brisk business in an open-air drug market, selling cocaine and smokable heroin to affluent young people from upscale neighborhoods. James takes another long drink. "What kinds of fools mess with drugs?" he wonders aloud.

Across town, Eleanor, an attorney, unwinds from a long day in court with a bottle of wine and the evening news. The lead story is another drive-by shooting in a low-income neighborhood. "Who cares?" Eleanor asks herself. Drug-related violence is an old story and not a problem in her affluent neighborhood.

Despite the economic gulf between them, James and Eleanor share a common bond: they are both addicted to alcohol. The intoxicating liquid that more than a hundred million Americans drink for pleasure, they drink from necessity. If unchecked, they will both drink themselves to an early, painful, and completely preventable death.

Only a small percentage of addicted drinkers, like James, live on the street. The rest are our neighbors. Some are infants born with

1

alcohol on their breath; some are grammar-school children. Others are among the millions of teenagers who bounce back and forth between alcohol and illegal drugs. A startling percentage are college-age binge drinkers, and a growing number are well-heeled baby boomers heading into retirement.

At the same time, loneliness, a sense of uselessness, and retirement communities where social drinking is the norm are sending thousands of unsuspecting senior citizens into late-onset alcoholism. Isolation makes it easy for aging adults to hide the amount of their alcohol consumption, and more than one grandparent has taken his or her first drink at sixty, only to be admitted within a few years to a hospital detoxification ward by a shocked and disbelieving family.

ALCOHOL AND DRUGS:
THE U.S.'S NUMBER ONE HEALTH PROBLEM

Many addicted drinkers combine alcohol with illegal or prescription drugs, creating a complicated cross-addiction for themselves and a substance-abuse nightmare for their communities. Substance abuse is the number one health problem in the United States, and the health costs related to drug and alcohol use exceed one trillion dollars a year. Alcohol and drug-related problems extend across all barriers of class, age, and race, and the affluent are as likely to become addicts as the poor.

Disparities in media coverage, law enforcement, and medical treatment perpetuate the mistaken identification of the nation's drug problem with inner-city youth and exacerbate the cultural ignorance that often separates racial and ethnic groups. This divisive trend is an often overlooked part of the enormous price America pays for the widespread abuse of alcohol and use of illegal drugs.

Sadly, often neither doctors, mental health professionals, nor faith leaders are equipped to respond effectively to this epidemic of addictive drinking. In the presence of untrained doctors, alcoholics are extraordinarily adept at disguising their real symptoms. I know of one addict who went to forty doctors, and all but two gave him inappropriate medication and failed to recognize his addiction. Counselors and therapists, pastors, rabbis, imams, and other faith leaders who are untaught in substance abuse can likewise fall victim to the addict's often uncanny ability to hide his or her addiction. Some may spend years addressing the symptoms of addiction without ever recognizing the underlying cause of their clients' distress.

Amid this general ineffectiveness, there is hope for addicted drinkers—and their friends and families. Our sense of helplessness about alcoholism may account for why the majority of alcoholics never enter treatment programs. But this pessimism overlooks the remarkable percentage of addicted drinkers who, *having received appropriate help*, are living sober, productive lives.

It is important to note that, while the focus of this book is alcoholism, the similarities between alcohol and other drug addictions are greater than their differences, and many, many people are addicted to both. The distinctions are primarily in physical effects, diagnostic tests, and medical management of withdrawal. Effective intervention and treatment methods are generally the same (with some modifications) for all addictive substances.

Our own journey from helplessness to effective action begins with an investigation into the causes of addiction. Why do people become alcoholics? Recent medical research provides some startling answers to this question and brings us face-to-face with a sobering fact: few of us, if any, can say, "It could never happen to me."

FAMILY LEGACY; WORLD EPIDEMIC

As a young boy growing up in East Africa, Moses was beaten routinely by his alcoholic father. His mother turned much of the family's millet crop into a potent home brew, and Moses was forced to scavenge for food.

With the help of a caring family friend, Moses went to school and eventually graduated from college. He became a devout Christian, married, and raised six children. Neither he nor his wife ever drank alcohol. "I don't want to see my children suffer like I did," Moses told a friend.

In the mid-1990s, while on a church mission, Moses was killed by a drunk driver. Over the next decade, three of his children became alcoholics. Two daughters were infected with AIDS because of the alcohol-related promiscuity of their husbands, and by the year 2005, more than twenty of Moses grandchildren were growing up in alcoholic homes.

The experience of Moses and his family is repeated in countless cities, towns, and villages around the globe. Alcoholism is one of the world's most serious public health problems, creating hardship and tragedy for hundreds of millions of people. For example:

- Alcoholism has helped lower the life expectancy of Russian men to 57 years—two decades shorter than in Western Europe.

- In South Africa, one in three urban males is addicted to alcohol.

- In Chile, 70 percent of workplace absenteeism is related to problem drinking.

- In Papua New Guinea, almost nine in ten fatal road accidents involve drivers or pedestrians who are drunk.

- In the United States, someone is killed by a drunk driver every twenty-four minutes.

With the exception of drunk-driving accidents, however, the high cost of alcohol abuse around the globe remains largely invisible. This cost includes addiction, chronic poor health, physical and sexual abuse, premature deaths from accidents, violent crimes, and AIDS. "For all the focus on illegal drugs, the number one cause of the spread of AIDS is alcohol," reported a recovering addict and activist. "Get drunk, get stupid, get AIDS."[1]

2

It Could Never Happen to Me

~

Nadia married a good man. Jack was a successful contractor, a kind husband and father, and he never forgot a birthday or anniversary. He coached soccer, led a Boy Scout troop, and attended church every Sunday.

Jack's stumbling block was alcohol. He drank steadily throughout the early years of his marriage and by his midforties was a full-blown alcoholic. This condition caused both Jack and Nadia enormous anguish. Every morning, in their prayer time together, they begged God to take away Jack's desire to drink. Every evening by six, Jack was drunk.

When Jack and Nadia first visited my office, Jack was drinking a fifth of vodka a day. A physical exam, including two simple diagnostic tests for addicted drinking, confirmed that he was in the late stages of alcoholism. I knew Jack was unlikely to recover without professional help, and I strongly urged him to enter an outpatient treatment center. I directed Nadia to Al-Anon, the 12-Step program for family members and friends of alcoholics. I also asked her to learn as much as she could about addictive drinking and its impact on families.

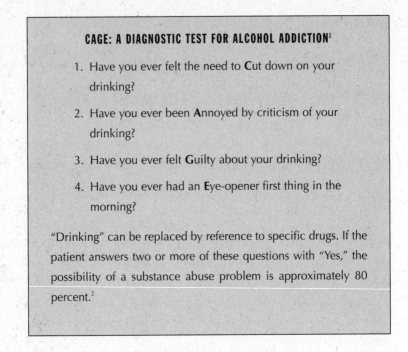

CAGE: A DIAGNOSTIC TEST FOR ALCOHOL ADDICTION[1]

1. Have you ever felt the need to **C**ut down on your drinking?
2. Have you ever been **A**nnoyed by criticism of your drinking?
3. Have you ever felt **G**uilty about your drinking?
4. Have you ever had an **E**ye-opener first thing in the morning?

"Drinking" can be replaced by reference to specific drugs. If the patient answers two or more of these questions with "Yes," the possibility of a substance abuse problem is approximately 80 percent.[2]

TAKE AS NEEDED FOR PAIN

Nadia, whose own father was an alcoholic, followed my advice. Jack consulted with his children and his minister and discovered that they were all as skeptical as he was about treatment programs. Once more, he decided to stop drinking on his own.

Two years later, during a heavy drinking episode, Jack had a heart attack. On his hospital bed, he realized that he was unable to stop drinking by his own devices and needed help. He agreed to enter treatment as soon as he was physically able, and he began educating himself about addiction.

One week after Jack's discharge, Nadia phoned to say that he had collapsed on the kitchen floor. When I arrived a few minutes later, Jack was dead.

After Jack's death, Nadia lived alone. Within a year her home was burglarized, and many of the possessions she and Jack had gathered together disappeared. Nadia plunged into a deep depression and could barely force herself out of bed each morning.

A psychiatrist wrote Nadia a prescription for a tranquilizer, and one evening, on her way home from work, she stopped by the store for a bottle of pink champagne. She took half a pill with a drink, and the tightness in her chest disappeared. For the first time in months, she slept soundly and woke up feeling refreshed.

Within six weeks, Nadia was drinking two glasses of champagne a night. During the workday, she hid her sadness from her coworkers behind a mask of indifference. At night, she rushed home to dissolve her grief in alcohol. "That bottle should have been labeled, 'Take as needed for pain,'" remembered Nadia. "It was better than any of my prescription drugs."

Nadia stopped attending her Thursday night book club, and she no longer returned phone calls from friends. With nothing to interfere with drinking, she progressed to three glasses of champagne a night. Occasionally she worried that she was picking up a bad habit, but her fears always disappeared with her first drink.

One evening, just a year after she started drinking, Nadia unintentionally downed an entire bottle of champagne. She became violently sick and collapsed on the floor. Sometime in the middle of the night, ashamed and afraid, she dragged herself to bed.

A DIVINE COINCIDENCE

Very early the next morning, I felt prompted to call Nadia and ask if she had a drinking problem. It was a "divine coincidence." Since Nadia's last physical, I had suspected that her isolation might be a symptom of alcohol abuse.

"The call came so early, I didn't have any makeup on," remembered Nadia. "Without that mask, it seemed easier to tell the truth. I regretted my honesty immediately, but by then it was too late."

I asked Nadia to come to my office, and there I gave her the same simple screening tests for alcoholism that I had given her husband. These tests confirmed what I intuitively knew: Nadia had become addicted to alcohol.

Nadia herself was convinced that she could not have become an alcoholic in such a short time, and for more than a year she tried multiple methods for controlling her drinking. She drank only wine; she drank only at night; she tried to limit herself to two drinks an evening. To her complete astonishment, she was never able to control the amount of alcohol she drank at any one sitting. She always drank until she was drunk.

Finally Nadia admitted that she could not stop drinking. "It was just so unacceptable to me to be addicted to alcohol," she recalled. "After growing up with an alcoholic father and then watching my husband's suffering, I couldn't believe that it had happened to me."

Today, by following a comprehensive program of recovery, Nadia no longer drinks. She has returned to her Thursday night book club, and she eats dinner once a week with a Single Again group. She is separated from her two-year drinking spree by nine years of sobriety, but occasionally she still feels an almost overwhelming urge for "one small drink." Such moments are an important reminder to Nadia of the reality of her addiction: in less than a year, she permanently crossed the line between moderate drinking and alcoholism.

Why do some people become alcoholics while others are able to drink moderately all their lives? It is a question that has puzzled medical researchers and laypeople for years, and the answers are not as simple as many of us have been led to believe.

3

Who's at Risk?

One hundred twenty million Americans drink alcoholic beverages; approximately 18 million, like Nadia, are alcoholics. Whether in a cocktail lounge, restaurant, private party, or living room, for every ten drinkers, there is likely to be at least one who cannot control the amount of alcohol he or she consumes.

The most popular explanations for this life-threatening dependence are psychological. Social drinkers, it is assumed, exercise self-control; alcoholics suffer from weakness of will. "I can't believe she let herself get into that shape!" "John can't hold his liquor." These frequently heard judgments question the alcoholic's character, implying that at best he lacks self-discipline; at worst, he is morally defective. In either case, the message is the same: "I would never let myself fall so far."

Biological and sociological explanations are often less condemning. Some people claim that there are physical problems peculiar to alcoholics, such as chemical imbalances or vitamin deficiencies. Others speculate that broken homes bequeath to children a vulnerability to addiction. Perhaps emotionally deprived children become love-starved adults whose only comfort is a bottle.

These theories, however morally satisfying or well-intentioned, are not supported by research. In fact, in many cases, the opposite of our popular assumptions has been shown to be true. For example:

1. *There is no preexisting "alcoholic personality."* People who work with alcohol addicts know there are many personality traits that show up with remarkable frequency. Alcoholics seem more dependent, self-centered, and oral (given to heavy smoking and/or compulsive talking/eating), and less self-controlled than nonalcoholics. The presence of these psychological similarities has given rise to speculation that insecure, dependent people are more likely to develop a drinking problem than those who are happy, well adjusted, and independent. However, a fascinating forty-five-year study by Dr. George Vaillant and his colleagues at Harvard University confirms what many alcoholism counselors have long suspected: the common emotional struggles of alcoholics are a *consequence*, not a *cause*, of addiction. If alcoholics appear to have similar psychological traits, it is because of the damaging effects of addictive drinking on human behavior.[1]

2. *Alcoholism has no known physical cause.* Many people have tried to prove through scientific experiments that addicts share a common physical ailment, such as allergies, liver disease, or blood-sugar disorders. So far, none of these popular notions about the physical causes of addiction have proven true. When alcoholics have common diseases and disorders, it is as a consequence of their addiction, not a cause.

3. *A broken home is not a primary cause of alcohol addiction.* Children who grow up in broken homes are at greater risk than their more fortunate peers for physical and emotional illness. Yet surprisingly, they are *not* at higher risk for alcoholism. "Alcoholics often

come from broken homes because their parents abused alcohol, not because broken homes cause alcoholism," reported Vaillant.[2]

Perhaps even more startling, *simply* growing up in an alcoholic home does not increase a child's risk of becoming an addicted drinker. In fact, studies show that, in the absence of alcoholism in their biological family, children adopted into alcoholic families have no increased risk for becoming addicted drinkers.[3]

Who, then, is at risk? While there are no known psychological, physical, or sociological problems common to all alcoholics, some of us have a greater chance of developing an addiction than others. The factors that put individuals and families at risk for alcoholism include:

THE FAMILY TREE

Multiple studies over a forty-year period have confirmed that alcoholism, or a susceptibility to addiction, is passed from generation to generation not by bad home environments but by genetic factors. The exact nature and extent of genetic influence on alcoholism is unknown, and the competing claims of researchers are difficult even for professionals to evaluate. For example, a recent highly publicized study convinced many people that there is a single gene for alcoholism, but a subsequent and less publicized evaluation called this research into serious question.[4]

If and when the exact genetic profile of alcoholism is discovered, it will likely be a family of genes, not a single gene, and these genes will not *cause* alcoholism but rather increase susceptibility to addiction. But as this complicated research unfolds, the bottom line remains simple: a genetic link to someone addicted to alcohol dramatically increases an individual's risk of alcoholism.

In light of this information, we all need to ask ourselves an important question: Is there an alcoholic in the house? Do we have a close relative—a mother, father, aunt, uncle, grandparent, sister, or brother—with a drinking problem?

The average social drinker, we have learned, has roughly a one-in-ten chance of developing an addiction to alcohol. With alcoholism in the family tree, social drinking begins to resemble Russian roulette. Virtually every alcoholic I have known echoes Nadia's story: the development of alcoholism is an unconscious drift toward addiction. By the time the genetically susceptible drinker is aware that she's in trouble, it's too late. She is caught in an addiction from which she cannot return without help.

ADOLESCENT DRINKERS AND BRAIN DAMAGE

Drinking and drunkenness among young people is often perceived by family members and friends as a harmless rite of passage whose consequences are more likely to be comical than tragic. In fact, one in two high-school seniors drink, and one in three report being drunk in the last month. Recent research, however, has shown that adolescents who binge drink may permanently damage their adult brains.[5] Early drinking is also a risk factor for alcoholism: two out of five adolescents who begin drinking by the age of fourteen will become addicted to alcohol.[6]

Parents who, in the presence of a family history of addictive drinking, are concerned about their children developing alcoholism might note that children of dogmatic teetotalers—those who take a rigid and alarmist attitude toward drinking—may be at unusually high risk for developing an addiction. An informative, non-alarmist approach is required. The "Letter to Grandchildren" in Appendix A is one example of a positive approach to children at risk.

When we consider the subtle nature of addiction and the infinite value of every individual life, those of us who drink and have alcoholism in our family tree must sensibly ask, is it worth it? Are the rewards of alcohol so great that they balance out the risk of developing an incurable addiction? If the answer is no, it's time to find an alternative method of relaxation. With a family history of addiction, my own medical recommendation is that abstinence is a sensible, responsible approach.

CRISES

Manuel retired at sixty-five from a long career as an executive in a textile plant. The sudden change from prestigious, time-consuming work to anonymous leisure left him feeling tired and depressed. A friend advised him to liven up his day with a splash of vodka in his morning orange juice. Manuel, never a regular drinker, began downing a "screwdriver" with breakfast.

Within a year, Manuel was drinking a fifth of whiskey a day. By the time his friend brought him to my office in a wheelchair, Manuel was the sickest elderly alcoholic I had ever seen. It was two months before he was able to walk with a cane and enter a treatment center.

Retirement, illness, divorce, death. No one is immune to these personal crises, which significantly increase our risk for alcohol addiction. Like Nadia or Manuel, we may be abstinent or moderate drinkers who find ourselves seeking comfort from alcohol during difficult days. At such times, regardless of our previous drinking habits and even in the absence of a family history of alcoholism, abstinence should be given serious consideration.

TRAUMA

Studies have consistently demonstrated a strong connection between alcohol abuse and many forms of trauma, including the suffering caused by child abuse, poverty, war, racism, and violent crime.

Many trauma victims begin to manifest a painful constellation of symptoms identified as post-traumatic stress disorder (PTSD). These symptoms include chronic anxiety, hyperarousal, and even hallucinations. For sufferers of PTSD, heavy drinking can be a cheap and temporary means of self-medication. Ironically, the alcoholism to which heavy drinking can lead is itself a severe form of trauma.

Because PTSD has turned out to be far more common and debilitating than previously thought, the connection between alcohol abuse and post-traumatic stress disorder is no small matter for the public health of any nation. "Exposure to extreme stress is widespread," reported Bessel A. van der Kolk, a Harvard psychiatrist and pioneer in the medical understanding of trauma. Of those exposed to extreme stress, "a substantial proportion" will develop PTSD.[7]

DUAL DIAGNOSIS: EMOTIONAL ILLNESS AND ALCOHOLISM

Individuals who suffer from emotional illness, such as depression, schizophrenia, bipolar disorder, or anxiety disorders, may in the presence of heavy drinking have a special vulnerability to addiction. Because of its numbing and sedating qualities, alcohol is often used as a form of self-medication by mentally ill adults and young people (and even children).

When self-medication leads to addiction, emotionally ill individuals can develop a seemingly hopeless, interwoven collection of physical and emotional problems. The prognosis for the dually diagnosed patient is far less optimistic than for individuals suffering from only addiction or only mental illness. At the same time, advances in the understanding and treatment of dually diagnosed patients have improved their chances of living sober and productive lives.

Sadly, sexually abused children from alcoholic homes exhibit more symptoms of post-traumatic stress disorder than any other trauma group. I have seen this countless times in my own medical practice, and a full 70 percent of our female patients at the Vanderbilt Institute for the Treatment of Addiction (VITA) report that they were sexually abused as children.

ETHNICITY AND CULTURE

"Drinking is the same all over the world." This was the informed judgment of a European alcoholism expert until he visited Gallup, New Mexico. There, on the border of a Navajo reservation, he found a town literally covered with alcoholics. Drunken adults and youths passed out on the street were almost as common as empty beer bottles scattered along the roadside. "There is something horrifying about the look of Navajo drinking in Gallup," wrote Calvin Trillin. "Something that makes it less like big-city skid-row drinking than like a medieval epidemic."[8]

Perhaps because of an inborn metabolic intolerance for alcohol, indigenous groups, such as Native Americans, the Inuit, and the Maori people of New Zealand, suffer disproportionate consequences from alcohol use and abuse. However, many Western industrialized countries are also at risk. France has the highest rate of cirrhosis of the liver in the world. In Canada, nine in ten violent crimes are committed under the influence of alcohol and/or illegal drugs.

In the United States, despite the attention given to crack cocaine and methamphetamine, alcohol is still the number one drug problem of all ethnic groups. The economic cost of alcohol abuse to the U.S. economy exceeds $160 billion a year. To put this figure in perspective, in 1998 the total retail sales of alcohol (beer, wine, and distilled spirits) were less than $110 billion.[9]

At the opposite end of the spectrum are Muslims, Mormons, Jews, and Italians. Observant Muslims and Mormons, who forbid the drinking of alcoholic beverages, have almost no alcoholism in their families. Jews and Italians also have surprisingly low rates of alcoholism. Jews in particular are frequent subjects for study; even though few practice total abstinence, few have developed alcoholism until recently, when more and more Jews have assimilated into Western culture.

COCAINE MYTHS

The average person thinks cocaine is the most dangerous drug in the United States. But by any measure, tobacco causes the most harm—430,000 related deaths per year, or one in every five deaths. Next is alcohol with 100,000 related deaths annually. Finally, there are illegal drugs, estimated to cause directly or indirectly about 25,000 deaths per year, and of these, perhaps 5,000 are attributed to cocaine.[10]

What separates cultures with high alcoholism rates from those with low rates? It is not, as is frequently supposed, biological or racial differences. The two most important factors are attitudes toward public drunkenness and whether or not drinking takes place outside of meals. *Nations and communities that drink only at the dinner table and do not tolerate public drunkenness do not have high rates of alcoholism.*[10]

When we examine American culture in light of these findings, the news is not encouraging. Americans habitually drink outside of meals and tolerate "party drunkenness" to such a degree that it is difficult to distinguish heavy drinkers from alcoholics. A medical student once told me, "There was no way my father could tell that my mother was an alcoholic because he was drinking so heavily himself." And an alcoholic patient reported, "I never needed to conceal my drinking, because all of my friends were doing the same thing. Too much drinking at parties was not just socially acceptable; it was the in thing to do."

This cultural inclination toward excessive consumption of alcohol is no minor social problem. Heavy drinking is to alcoholism what smoking is to lung cancer—an effective, reliable means of developing a terminal illness. Even in the absence of a personal crisis or an inherited predisposition, heavy drinking can lead almost anyone, at any time of life, into alcoholism.

The connection between heavy drinking and addiction has profound implications not just for our society, but for each of us individually. It brings us face-to-face with an important and personal question: How much is too much?

4

How Much Is Too Much?

I know my limit." This is the bold claim made by heavy drinkers who consistently drink all their friends under the table. It is repeated by social drinkers who stop at one or two drinks and by people who choose not to drink at all. Other people may have drinking problems, but we ourselves are certain we know when to quit.

Is there a safe amount of alcohol a person can drink? There is no known answer. The amount of alcohol that will lead a given individual into addiction is impossible to determine; there are simply too many variables. Nonetheless, the following information can provide helpful parameters.

1. *There may be "instant addicts."* For reasons still unknown, there are some people who seem profoundly affected by alcohol from the very first drink. These individuals report that they virtually never had the opportunity to drink socially; they were almost immediately out of control of their drinking.

Marty Mann told the story of one such addict, an eighty-year-old matriarch of a prominent New England family. Following her doctor's advice, the elderly woman took her first drink at the age of seventy-nine and immediately began raiding the family liquor closet. "Terrible tales came back to plague the family pride—of mayhem in public bars, of teetering progress down the main street with a bottle tucked under each arm, of agitated policemen . . . [The family] took the only possible out, and when last heard of, the old lady was enjoying herself in a good sanitarium where the kindly doctors allowed her four drinks a day, and she spent her time conniving to get five or six."[1]

2. *Heavy drinking, or frequent drunkenness, is a major factor in addiction.* Any person who regularly drinks heavily or to the point of intoxication is placing him- or herself in a high-risk category for developing alcoholism. The standard for heavy drinking depends on gender, as well as body weight and metabolism rates. In general, heavy drinking for men is defined as three to four drinks on a single occasion, and for women, two to three. For some people, one drink can lead to intoxication. *Even in the absence of an inherited, genetic susceptibility, heavy regular drinking over a period of time can lead virtually anyone into addiction.*

In the presence of a family history of alcoholism, heavy drinking takes on the character of a suicide wish, and sooner or later, it is likely to demand payment. With an alcoholic father, Nadia, whom we met in Chapter 2, became an addict in a year. Others with alcoholism in their family tree drink for ten, twenty, or even thirty years before losing control of their drinking.

With or without a family history of addiction, heavy drinking is *always* high-risk drinking. No matter how many years a heavy drinker successfully avoids addiction, with each passing year, she increases her chances of becoming an alcoholic.

3. *There are no safe forms of alcohol.* The person who says he can't be an alcoholic because he only drinks beer is fooling himself, but not his liver. Some of the most badly damaged livers I've ever seen belonged to beeraholics who were astonished to learn that they had been killing themselves with six-packs. These individuals were certain

that beer was less dangerous than whiskey or vodka, or even wine. The truth is that the alcohol content in a 12-ounce can of beer is equal to that in a 5-ounce glass of wine or a mixed drink with 1.5 ounces of 80 proof distilled spirits. The simplified formula is easy to remember: one 12-ounce can of beer = one 5-ounce glass of wine = one mixed drink.

4. *There is no safe amount of alcohol.* The amount of alcohol a person can drink without becoming intoxicated depends on his or her size, sex, age, and metabolism. Most women, for example, become intoxicated more quickly than men, in part because they have lower levels of an enzyme that helps digest alcohol. Nadia was drinking heavily at two glasses of champagne a day, and I have known patients who were regularly intoxicated on one beer or a glass of wine.

Regardless of the kind or amount of alcohol consumed, or whether addiction sets in quickly or over a period of many years, the end result is the same. Once a person is addicted to alcohol, he has set in motion forces over which he no longer has control. As the following story illustrates, the alcoholic is trapped in a complex and finely woven web of compulsive drinking.

JOURNEY INTO DESPAIR

Dr. Jordan was sixteen years old when he drank his first hard liquor. The year was 1961, he was a guest at a debutante ball, and the beverage was a home brew mixed with fruit punch. After one drink, Jordan's natural shyness seemed to disappear. After two, he felt unusually witty and exceptionally graceful. By midnight, he was badly intoxicated. He drove himself and his friends home at dangerously high speeds and in the morning had a severe hangover. It seemed a small and grown-up price to pay for an evening of social success.

Fourteen years later, Jordan was a well-established family doctor in the Midwest. He had married his high-school sweetheart, and they had four children. An active church member, Jordan took time from his busy practice to sing in the choir and teach a popular teen Sunday school class.

Since Jordan's high-school years, his drinking habits had changed several times. He joined the army at eighteen and for three years drank sporadically but heavily. In college, he got drunk every Saturday with his fraternity brothers, but in medical school, he stopped drinking altogether. In his thirties, as a married man with a substantial income, he began drinking on weekends with golfing friends.

Over the next ten years, Jordan increased his drinking to three or four times a week and occasionally became drunk on weekends. Jordan's wife strongly opposed his drinking, and while he resented her interference, he frequently stopped drinking for months at a time.

In his midforties, Jordan began to drink every day. He poured himself a drink as soon as he came home from work and frequently had two or three more in the evening. His wife was alarmed by this change in his drinking habits and finally left him. Because Jordan valued his marriage more than his vodka, he substantially cut back on his drinking, and his wife moved back home.

A year later, Jordan's wife was seriously injured in a car accident, and passed away shortly thereafter. Jordan was left alone to care for his children, a large house, and an enormous medical practice.

Burdened by loneliness and new responsibilities, Jordan stepped up his drinking. Every evening he returned home from his hospital rounds, prepared dinner, and poured himself a large glass of vodka. He drank three or four glasses before going to bed and often fell sleep in the living room.

Within two years of his wife's accident, Jordan was drinking more than a gallon of vodka a week. He became increasingly frightened by his heavy consumption and several times stopped drinking for weeks at a time. During these periods, his desire for alcohol was an overwhelming, almost physical presence in his life. At every waking moment, he was consciously *not* drinking. This minute-by-minute battle exhausted Jordan's physical and mental resources, and when a television beer commercial or careless dose of cough syrup finally broke his resistance, he felt enormous relief. It was only *when* he was drinking that he could think about something other than alcohol.

By now, Jordan was suffering from high blood pressure, chronic diarrhea, a stomach ulcer, arm and leg pain, and the morning "shakes." He could barely hold his toothbrush, and every morning the taste of toothpaste caused him to vomit in the sink.

While mornings were difficult, it was his medical practice that was the biggest problem. "You can't imagine the work it takes to be an alcoholic and carry on a demanding job," said Jordan. "When I was working, I never drank before five thirty in the evening, but I was always nauseated and sick and fighting a terrible desire to drink. I could hardly think, yet I had to function at an extremely high level."

Thanks to mentholated cough drops and a well-meaning medical partner, none of Jordan's friends or patients knew he had a drinking problem. On emergency nighttime call, however, he began minimizing the seriousness of his patients' symptoms so that he would not have to drive while intoxicated. He also frequently prescribed medications or made diagnoses of which he had no memory in the morning. He blamed his lapses on fatigue; sympathetic nurses and medical technicians covered for his mistakes.

Every Sunday Jordan sent his children to Mass, although he himself rarely attended. "It was just too painful," explained Jordan. "I envied the people there, and I sincerely wanted to give my life to God, but it was no longer mine to give."

One day, a woman (whose elderly mother Jordan had neglected during a nighttime emergency) stopped him on the street to ask about his sad appearance. Jordan replied bluntly. "My problem is alcohol. I can't stop drinking."

Jordan's unexpected revelation led to a prayer service at his church, and he experienced an immediate desire to stop drinking. A few months later, I met Jordan at a medical conference. When I heard his story, I suggested that he consider admitting himself to a treatment program for impaired physicians.

Jordan was convinced that he would never drink again, but as a precautionary measure he followed my advice. Several months later, seemingly from out of nowhere, his desire to drink returned with crushing intensity. By then Jordan was surrounded by a strong support system, and for the first time in his life, he resisted his craving for alcohol.

Today Jordan is sober. His friends and patients wonder why he looks ten years younger, and Jordan is still astonished to wake up every morning to the absence of pain. "My head doesn't hurt, my hands don't shake, and there is no boring pain in my stomach. I never thought I would feel this good again."

Like millions of other recovering alcoholics, Jordan stays sober "one day at a time." "Alcohol is patient," Jordan said. "It waits for you. As the months go by, things get easier, but every once in a while, I still get an almost overwhelming desire for 'just one more drink.'"

Jordan is one of thousands of physicians who have permanently crossed the line between social drinking and alcoholism. These doctors, along with millions of other alcoholics, no longer drink to feel good; they drink to feel normal. In many cases, they are knowingly drinking themselves to death, but like Jordan, they are more afraid of not drinking than of dying.

What is this strange and baffling disorder that causes so many of our best and brightest citizens to destroy themselves? A bad habit? A weakness in the will? A disease?

To answer these questions, it is helpful to learn a few basic facts about alcohol and the nature of addiction.

5

Abuse—or Addiction?

~

Alcohol," wrote George Bernard Shaw, "makes life bearable to millions of people who could not endure their existence if they were quite sober. It enables Parliament to do things at eleven at night that no sane person would do at eleven in the morning."[1]

For hundreds of years, alcohol has been the traditional "high" of many countries and cultures. Its widespread use and acceptance, as well as legality, have served to mask an important fact: alcohol is an addicting drug.

Medically speaking, alcohol is an irregularly descending depressant of the central nervous system. In plain English, it interferes in progressive and predictable stages with the normal control functions of the brain.

In small amounts, even one drink or less, alcohol acts on the part of the brain that controls inhibitions. It relaxes or removes the restraints that govern behavior, giving the drinker a sense of euphoria and well-being. This release of the emotions from their normal controls, or *mood-altering* effect, frequently causes alcohol to be mislabeled as a *stimulant*. In fact, it is a *depressant*, which slows down the intellect and other bodily functions.

In larger quantities, alcohol depresses the cerebellum and interferes with the body's balance mechanism. The drinker begins to stagger, and his speech becomes slurred. Because his judgment is seriously impaired, the drinker is usually unaware that he can no longer properly walk—or drive. For most men, two and a half drinks (approximately three to four ounces of alcohol) in one hour are more than enough to make driving a risky business. For some women, one drink can cause impaired judgment.

In large quantities, alcohol anesthetizes the brain stem, the body's control center for respiration and heartbeat. A fifth of whiskey in one hour is enough to completely paralyze the brain stem of most drinkers and send them into an alcoholic coma. Despite a great deal of recent publicity, this lethal effect of alcohol remains relatively unacknowledged. Every year a tragic number of high-school and college students are brought to hospital emergency rooms, dead on arrival, because they accepted the challenge to chug a six-pack of beer or a fifth of vodka.

As a toxic drug that requires no digestion, alcohol is distributed uniformly throughout body tissues and cells. The rate of absorption depends on how much food is in the stomach and how much alcohol is in the beverage. The higher the concentration of alcohol, the more quickly the alcohol is absorbed by the body—whiskey has more "kick" than beer. Alcohol is removed from the body primarily through the liver, the body's detoxification plant, and on average, this process takes about an hour and a half per can of beer, glass of wine, or mixed drink.[2]

THE BIOLOGY OF CRAVING

Why is alcohol addicting? New research suggests that, when consumed in large amounts, alcohol produces long-term changes in the reward system of the brain. These complex and perhaps irreversible changes decrease the pleasure an alcoholic gets from drinking, while at the same time increasing his craving.[3] Like Dr. Jordan, addicted drinkers end up needing more and more alcohol, not to feel good, but to *not* feel, for at least a few moments each day, their urgent and often despair-filled craving for alcohol.

Addiction is a complex interplay of physical, emotional, social, and spiritual factors, but it is this physical dependence on alcohol that enables us to distinguish, at least in theory, between people who are simply drinking too much—alcohol abusers—and people who cannot control their drinking—alcohol addicts.

I WOULD DO ANYTHING

It's hard for a person who isn't addicted to drugs or alcohol to understand the power of craving. But imagine you are twenty feet under water, and you've just run out of breath. You'll do anything to get to the surface. Anything. That's what it feels like when I need a drink.

—CHERYL

THE ALCOHOL ABUSER

For most of his adult life, Dr. Jordan was not an alcoholic. He was a heavy drinker, an alcohol *abuser*. From the age of sixteen, when he first discovered the joys of intoxication, Jordan rarely drank less than four or five drinks at a sitting. He enjoyed the mood-altering effect of heavy drinking, and as circumstances permitted, he drank more and more frequently.

Like most alcohol abusers, Jordan could choose when he drank, how much he drank, or even if he drank. When his wife left him for several months, she raised the price of intoxication beyond what he was willing to pay. The painful consequences of excessive drinking suddenly outweighed its pleasures, and Jordan was able to cut back on his drinking.

Thousands, perhaps millions, of alcohol abusers have similar experiences every year. A young woman drinks too much at a sorority party, vomits all over her dress, and wakes up in the morning with distressing memories. The brief euphoria of drunkenness is forgotten in the pain of social embarrassment, and she decides never to drink heavily again. A respected member of the community gets drunk on New Year's Eve, has an accident, and receives a drunk-driving citation. His family is angry, he pays a stiff fine, and he vows that he has had his last drink. Perhaps he never has another alcohol-related problem.

HEAVY DRINKERS AND BRAIN DAMAGE

Intellectual impairment is one of the earliest consequences of alcoholism. But even in the absence of addiction, heavy drinkers experience grave consequences from drinking. According to a recent and surprising study conducted by my friend and colleague, Dr. Peter R. Martin at Vanderbilt University, heavy drinkers experience the same pattern of brain damage as severe alcoholics, and they can be just as impaired in their daily function. Men averaging only one hundred drinks a month and women only eighty (less than three drinks a day) had significant impairment in their memory, learning, reading, and balance. Because these drinkers were still functioning normally, they did not recognize their need for medical help.[4]

THE ALCOHOL ADDICT

For the alcohol addict, however, the problems never end. The alcoholic cannot predict *when* or *how much* she will drink, and she continues to drink even after alcohol causes trouble in one or more areas of her life—family, friends, health, career, finances, or legal matters. Unlike the alcohol abuser, the alcohol addict is no longer in control of her own will. Her internal center for decision making and free choice has been captured by alcohol, and she is unable to choose not to drink.

This loss of self-control is extremely difficult for social drinkers and abstainers to understand. It is tempting to dismiss alcoholism as a problem unique to weak-minded people, but strong determination is no defense against addiction. I have watched more than one stubborn, strong-willed person involuntarily drink him- or herself to death, and the only significant difference I have ever noticed between seemingly strong and weak personalities is that strong-willed alcoholics pursue their drinking more aggressively.

Because alcohol addiction is only one point—the extreme end—on the whole spectrum of alcohol abuse, it's impossible to determine exactly when heavy drinking ends and addiction begins. Jordan was an alcohol abuser until his wife's accident. Shortly afterward, he was an alcoholic. It took him thirty years of heavy drinking to cross the line into addiction, but for his entire adult life, he was only a short step from trouble.

The euphoria that compels a heavy drinker to risk embarrassment or serious accident is only a distant memory for the alcoholic. He still depends on alcohol to alter his mood, but now he drinks primarily to numb his pain, not to feel good. The constant physical agitation of addictive craving combines with paralyzing guilt and self-hatred to trap the alcoholic in a chronic state of mental anguish. Even the most stalwart individual cannot live in this state indefinitely. With relief as close as the nearest bottle, the alcoholic, whether he consciously chooses to drink or not, inevitably finds himself intoxicated.

BINGE DRINKING

Contrary to popular belief, it is not necessary to drink day and night to be an alcoholic. One of the most baffling forms of alcoholism is binge drinking, a form of addiction in which the drinker gets drunk weekly or monthly but is sober many more days than he or she is drunk.

Binge drinking is often defined as consuming five or more drinks on one occasion for males and four or more drinks for women, but as we have seen, the point of intoxication differs remarkably from individual to individual. For many alcoholics, the period of time between binges becomes increasingly shorter, but this is not always the case. Even long-term addicts can experience periods of sobriety of two years or more, and many alcoholics periodically quit drinking in an attempt to prove to themselves and/or their families that they are normal drinkers. Sooner or later, however, the test period ends, and the alcoholic is once again involuntarily drinking to intoxication.

COLLEGE BINGE DRINKING

Among college students, one in two young men and two in five young women are binge drinkers. One of every four college students are frequent binge drinkers, drinking to intoxication three or more times in a fourteen-day period. Binge drinkers place themselves at high risk for not only the development of alcoholism but also for sudden injury and death.[6]

Not all binge drinking, as many a college student has shown, is a sign of addiction. But all binge drinking is dangerous and irresponsible. Binge drinking is the cause of untold numbers of fires, drownings, fatal falls, suicides, and murders, and it is a major reason why traffic accidents remain the single greatest cause of death among teenagers and young adults in the United States. Disturbingly, binge drinking is currently the number one health problem on most college campuses, and the social culture surrounding binge drinking is so central to student life that many experts believe it cannot be curtailed.[5]

IS ALCOHOLISM A DISEASE—OR A SIN?

When doctors and mental health workers refer to alcoholism as a disease, many people get understandably nervous. They see the disease label as a psychiatric sleight of hand, an attempt to deny the willful wrong behavior of heavy drinkers and excuse the alcoholic from responsibility for his or her actions.

In my own Christian tradition, as well as for Jews and Muslims, alcohol abuse and drunkenness are clearly immoral. While contemporary Western society accepts intoxication within limits (for example, it's all right to be drunk at a party, but not behind the wheel), the sacred texts of the world's major religions forbid drunkenness altogether. In the Bible, the apostle Paul said, "The acts of the sinful nature are obvious: sexual immorality, impurity and debauchery; idolatry and witchcraft; hatred, discord, jealousy, fits of rage, selfish ambition, dissensions, factions and envy; drunkenness, orgies, and the like. I warn you, as I did before, that those who live like this will not inherit the kingdom of God" (Galatians 5:19–21).

It's not hard to understand why Paul spoke so strongly. Alcohol abuse is a major factor in a high percentage of murders and suicides, in physical and sexual assaults on children, in traffic fatalities, and in fire and drowning accidents. It is also the primary cause of alcohol *addiction.* Clearly, we do ourselves and our entire society a great disservice when we laugh at drunkenness or treat it lightly.

While the alcohol abuser chooses to get drunk, the alcoholic drinks involuntarily. Her willpower is in service to her addiction, and she cannot resist her craving for alcohol. Telling an alcohol addict to shape up and stop drinking is like telling a person who jumps out of a nine-story building to fall only three floors. Words will not alter the inevitable outcome.

Because of the alcoholic's helplessness, and because addiction generally follows a predictable pattern and has a pronounced inheritance factor, it is not inappropriate to call alcoholism a "disease." But addiction to any substance is never simply a *physical* disease; rather, addiction is the paradigm disease of the *whole* person. While an individual with diabetes or cancer can possess a healthy mind and emotions, as well as deep friendships and family ties, the alcoholic is at risk to lose everything. He is sick in his body, mind, emotions, spirit, and relationships. Unless the addicted drinker gets help in all these areas, his chances for recovery are very poor indeed.

"First the person takes a drink, then the drink takes a drink, then the drink takes the person." This ancient proverb says it well. Whatever label we attach to alcoholism, addiction has a life of its own. The heavy drinker has set in motion powerful forces over which she has no control, and she begins to exhibit the predictable but often unrecognized symptoms of addiction.

6

Early Warning Signs

⌁

"The earlier the diagnosis, the better the prognosis." This simple medical principle applies to alcoholism as aptly as it does to cancer or heart disease. Statistically, the earlier we identify an addiction, the more likely it is that the alcoholic will recover.

The opposite is also true. The longer we wait to diagnose alcoholism, the poorer the alcoholic's chances for recovery. Alcohol addiction is most often a progressive, chronic, and comprehensive disorder. If left to run its course, it gets worse, not better. The longer an alcoholic drinks, the more completely he destroys himself. When finally he has lost his personality, family, friends, health, and job, the alcoholic is terminally ill and has little incentive for living, much less staying sober.

The importance of recognizing the early warning signs of addiction cannot be overemphasized. Unfortunately, the best-known symptoms of alcoholism are physical problems that occur in the late stages of addiction: red face, bulbous nose, and cirrhosis of the liver. Less understood but vastly more important are the behavior problems and early physical signs of addiction. Not every alcoholic manifests every symptom, but there is a predictable pattern of behavior that can be recognized by alert doctors, family members, friends, and employers.

THE SICKNESS OF THE SPIRIT

Long before alcohol abusers become alcoholics, they begin to experience the spiritual damage of heavy drinking. Heavy drinking not only interferes with faith commitments and spiritual practices such as prayer and meditation, but it can also lead the drinker to violate his or her own moral principles. Alcohol impairs the brain's judgment center, located in the frontal lobe. At the same time, as a mood-altering drug, it acts directly on the brain to depress or remove our built-in prohibitions against certain kinds of behavior. We depend on these inhibitions more than we want to believe, and when we combine a lack of inhibition with the absence of good judgment, we are subject to control by the specific weaknesses of our own particular character—anger, self-pity, greed, hatred, violence, lust, indolence.

A married man or woman with perfectly fine family values might drink too much, become euphoric, and go to bed with a casual acquaintance. When the alcohol wears off, he or she is left with deep feelings of guilt and shame. If the wrongdoing is not addressed, these feelings may be suppressed, but the memory of immoral behavior chips away at the drinker's already damaged moral life.

Once an individual has crossed the line into alcoholism, the drinker's moral struggles are likely to become more pronounced. He may repeatedly violate his own sense of right and wrong by telling petty lies, cheating at work, hiding bottles, stealing, and verbally or physically abusing other members of his family. In cases closer to home than many of us realize, alcoholism plays a role in spousal abuse, child abuse, and other violent crimes.

However immoral and unpredictable the actions of the alcoholic become, his conscience is never fully soluble in alcohol, and he is often tormented by guilt. "It is impossible to describe the emotional pain experienced by an alcoholic," said Dr. Jordan. "No matter how arrogant or self-confident he may seem, his primary emotions are shame and self-hatred."

Burdened by self-condemnation, most alcoholics drop out of active participation in their faith community. They may dismiss people of faith as hypocrites while secretly envying their appearance of respectability. A few alcoholics continue to attend religious services, but no matter how sincere their intentions, their spiritual lives are devoid of power.

No alcoholic can survive indefinitely the spiritual isolation and self-loathing generated by addiction. A tragic number of alcoholics eventually choose to kill themselves; the suicide rate among alcoholics is significantly higher than that of the general population.[1] The majority of alcoholics, however, survive long enough to drink themselves to death. To stay alive, they make use of the sophisticated defenses that enable all of us to deny unpleasant realities and protect ourselves from pain and suffering.

THE SICKNESS OF THE MIND AND EMOTIONS

Early in the addiction process, the alcoholic moves from *anticipation* to *preoccupation* with drinking. She no longer simply looks forward to drinking; she thinks about it most of the time. Her mental and emotional energies are redirected toward protecting her right to drink and living with her declining self-esteem. Accordingly, she begins to exhibit the predictable behavior symptoms of addiction.

RATIONALIZATION AND PROJECTION

"I always had a convincing reason to drink," remembered a forty-five-year-old alcoholic patient. "First I drank to be social. Then I drank to relax after work. Next I drank to sleep. Finally I drank to forget. None of these explanations seemed to be rationalizations at the time. I had real needs, and I was convinced that only alcohol could meet them."

As the alcoholic's addiction progresses, her need for alcohol increases. She begins to drink more frequently and to plan her day around drinking. She often hides bottles at home or at work and becomes irritated when unexpected schedule changes delay her drinking.

As the alcoholic's behavior grows increasingly rigid, her rationalizations often become more and more pathological. Through subtle criticism or shocking accusations, she may project her self-hatred onto the people closest to her. She may blame her drinking on her husband's work schedule, her children's ungratefulness, or her boss's unfairness. Eventually the alcoholic's accusations may become so bizarre and hate-filled that family relationships and friendships are permanently damaged or destroyed.

The alcoholic has an uncanny ability to convince others that they are responsible for her drinking, and it is family members who are most vulnerable to her accusations. Pushed to the breaking point by the alcoholic's unpredictable behavior, many spouses of alcoholics seek psychiatric help—for themselves. One wife of an alcoholic was in an outpatient mental health clinic for several weeks before doctors realized that she was there because her husband had convinced her that she was crazy.

MOOD SWINGS AND PERSONALITY CHANGES

While the alcoholic is increasingly critical of the people around her, her own behavior is, at best, unpredictable. She becomes irritable and defensive, and her mood may change from jubilant euphoria to angry suspicion in a matter of minutes. These mood swings are particularly pronounced when the alcoholic is "on the wagon" or attempting to cut back on her drinking.

At the extreme end of mood swings is the "Dr. Jekyll and Mr. Hyde syndrome." For reasons not yet known, some people undergo a dramatic personality change when they are drinking. This transformation closely resembles the presence of two personalities in one body, and for family members it is one of the most terrifying aspects of alcoholism. A spouse, parent, or child disappears, and in his or her place is a total stranger who may appear devoid of conscience.

One middle-aged individual was a highly moral man who, while drinking, watched pornographic movies in front of his children. Another patient, a bank executive and prominent church member, was unusually considerate and charming to his family until he had a few drinks. Then anything could happen. He spent one European vacation roaming the streets in his underwear, knocking on doors and challenging local residents to a fight. His children hid behind a barricaded door, terrified that he would carry out his threats to return and kill them.

The bizarre nature of the Jekyll and Hyde syndrome leads some religious people to speculate that alcoholism is a consequence of demon possession, of a "spirit" of alcoholism that invades the bodies of alcoholics. Anyone who has witnessed firsthand an alcohol- or drug-induced personality change can understand this fear. At the same time, we must not underestimate the toxic effects of chronic drinking. The disturbing truth is that alcohol and other powerful mood-altering drugs can produce schizophrenic personality changes in human beings.

BLACKOUTS

Many alcoholics have times when they function normally, never lose consciousness, and yet have no memory of where they have been or what they have done. This chemically induced amnesia is called a *blackout*. Sermons have been preached, cross-continental flights flown, heart surgeries performed, and military operations executed by people who have no memory of their experience. "When I remember the many nights I made diagnoses or prescribed drugs in an alcoholic blackout, I know it's only by God's grace that I never killed anyone," said Dr. Jordan.

Other alcoholics are not so fortunate. One friend of mine slammed into the back of a car and permanently crippled an elderly driver. Another driver, a real estate broker, called his doctor early one morning. "They tell me that last night I drove my car through three kids on bicycles and killed one," he said. "I don't remember . . ." It was a lost memory with which the broker couldn't live. The night before his trial, he killed himself.[2]

BLACKOUT

The exact physical mechanism of an alcoholic blackout is unknown, but it is likely to be related to alcohol's damaging effect on the delicate chemistry of long- and short-term memory storage. The time frame covered by a memory loss can be minutes—or months. One alcoholic, a corporate executive, spent a week at a convention center, drinking and conducting high-level financial transactions. She returned to her home office only to discover that she had no memory of any agreements that she had made. Another patient, a professor, has only a handful of memories from the last twenty years of his life. He has severely damaged his short-term memory and can no longer follow even a simple set of directions.

SOCIAL CHANGES

The alcoholic frequently begins his drinking career as "the life of the party." By the time his addiction has progressed to recognizable stages, however, his old friends have usually disappeared. His intoxicated behavior is no longer amusing as he becomes increasingly critical and angry toward nonalcoholics. The alcoholic narrows his social circle to people with whom he can drink heavily without embarrassment. If he has to attend a party where alcohol is not served, usually he has several drinks beforehand to fortify himself for the ordeal.

The family life of the alcoholic, for reasons we will examine later, is usually hidden from the public eye. However, as his drinking continues, the alcoholic often complains of marriage problems, sexual frustrations, and financial difficulties. Sometimes there are sudden or unexplained changes in the family structure, such as separation or divorce, or children leaving home at early ages to live with relatives.

Although friends and family members experience the alcoholic's strange behavior early in his addiction, the alcoholic takes great pains to conceal his problem at work. Sooner or later, however, his job performance begins to deteriorate. He shows up late for work on Monday mornings or after holidays and has an increased number of unexplained absences. He finds it hard to concentrate for extended periods of time, and he may become increasingly moody or aggressive toward his fellow workers. Both the volume and the quality of his work may begin to fall to substandard levels.

PHYSICAL SYMPTOMS

While the earliest symptoms of alcohol addiction are behavior patterns, before long the alcoholic begins to pay a physical price for his addiction. Early physical symptoms include night sweats, morning nausea and vomiting, diarrhea, gastritis (inflammation of the stomach lining), hand tremors, a slightly enlarged or tender liver, and in men, impotence. Frequently, the alcoholic also has unexplained bruises or cigarette burns on his body.

As the alcoholic's addiction progresses, his physical problems become more serious. His face flushes, his nose may become inflamed and enlarged, his palms may turn red ("liver palms"), and he can suffer from any of dozens of medical complications: high blood pressure, ulcers, pancreatitis, heart disease, cirrhosis, kidney failure, esophageal cancer, anemia, tuberculosis, irreparable brain damage, and so on. In men, alcohol damage to the liver can raise estrogen levels. As a result, their testicles shrink, their breasts grow, and they may permanently lose the ability to have an erection. For both men and women, a complete list of alcohol-related medical problems reads much like a summary of everything that can go wrong with the human body.

By the late stages of addiction, the alcoholic's central nervous system has adjusted to the constant presence of alcohol. If his blood-alcohol level drops unexpectedly, he experiences withdrawal symptoms: rapid pulse, severe headaches, the shakes (involuntary trembling of the head, limbs, and tongue), and in the most serious cases, *delirium tremens* (DT's). This "pink elephant" stage, despite its humorous reputation, is a nightmarish phenomenon that kills a disturbing number of its victims. The alcoholic is mentally tortured by his poisoned, malfunctioning brain, and his uncontrollable screaming is deeply unsettling even for the most experienced of medical staff. One of my alcoholic patients was convinced for hours that he was being attacked by monstrous dogs leaping from tree limbs, and no one could persuade him otherwise. Another patient, whose addiction was missed in a medical history, went through life-threatening alcohol withdrawal while recovering from back surgery. When I was called in for a consultation, the patient grabbed my hand. "Mr. Death was just here, dressed in black," she told me, shaking uncontrollably. "He rolled the dice and said I wasn't going to make it. Please, please make him come back and roll again." The patient survived, but only after hours of inconsolable terror.

With his health and personality deteriorating, his job in jeopardy, and his relationships heading to ruin, the alcoholic is desperately in need of help. Strangely, the longer his addiction continues and the bigger the price he pays for drinking, the less able he is to see himself as sick.

PERMANENT BRAIN DAMAGE

In the final stages of addiction, the alcoholic often suffers permanent brain damage. Years of heavy drinking deplete the body's supply of thiamine, an essential vitamin for growth and maintenance of nerve tissue, and the alcoholic's brain begins to shrink. As the brain shrinks, the ventricles that bathe the brain in spinal fluid expand to fill the empty space. The result is "water brain." One of my patients, a Renaissance man and research scientist, spent the last thirty years of his life in a wheelchair, and the X-ray evidence of the shrinking and watering of his brain was painful to observe.

7

"Don't Call Me an Alcoholic!"

⌒

I t was during Ben's first visit to his family doctor that he heard the good news: he was not an alcoholic. "You're under a lot of stress," the doctor told him. "But give yourself time. Work things out with your wife, and try not to drink so much."

Ben was happy to hear a professional confirm what he had tried to tell his wife for months. The doctor gave him a prescription for an antianxiety drug, and Ben celebrated by joining friends for golf. By four o'clock he was working on his third half-pint, and by six o'clock he had passed out on a green. His friends were gone when he woke up, so he drove himself home, hitting a stop sign on the way.

Ben, a successful engineer who had once studied to become a minister, had been drinking for thirteen years. "From the very beginning, I was unusually affected by alcohol," he remembered.

Ben began as a binge drinker whose drinking episodes were separated by weeks, and sometimes even months. When he reached his early forties, his drinking pattern reversed. Now he stayed drunk for weeks at a time, sobering up only for major projects. When he wasn't drinking, he functioned reasonably well; drunk, he was unpredictable and dangerous. One night, Ben hit his wife, Belinda, and broke her nose; another evening, he challenged his son to a fistfight. At work, he began to verbally abuse his colleagues and clients and even threatened his company with a lawsuit.

Belinda was increasingly frightened by Ben's behavior and went to their family doctor for help. The doctor had little experience with alcoholism but directed Belinda to Al-Anon, which she began to attend. Belinda also began leaving information about alcoholism around the house, hoping Ben would read it.

One afternoon, in a state of sober depression, Ben decided to attend Alcoholics Anonymous. He was escorted from his first meeting because he was drunk, but someone gave him a copy of AA's "Big Book." He spent the next week drinking and reading the testimonials of recovering alcoholics. "I thought if I could avoid their mistakes, then I wouldn't become an alcoholic," Ben remembered.

The following year, when Ben's daughter was married, he spent the two weeks prior to her wedding in an alcoholic blackout. He lived in a hotel room, seemed to function normally, yet had no memory of more than ten days of his life. He sobered up in time for the wedding, but at the reception experienced severe hallucinations from withdrawal. While his family danced and celebrated, Ben was attacked by disfigured creatures crawling out of the walls, laughing and shrieking and offering him pints of vodka.

A year later, Ben decided to enter an inpatient treatment program. After two days of detoxification and three days into the program, he was convinced he wasn't an alcoholic. "I became a counselor instead," Ben remembered. "Because of my seminary experience, many patients looked to me for spiritual expertise, and I was only too happy to help them."

The turning point for Ben came when one of his "patients" left the treatment center on a confident, upbeat note and was drunk before she reached her own doorstep. When Ben heard the news, he began crying uncontrollably.

"It was like I was in an alcoholic blackout," Ben remembered. "When I came to, I was lying under my bed, weeping. Until then, I thought I was only crazy when I was drinking, but by then I hadn't had a drink for twenty-one days.

"All of a sudden I knew I was insane. What normal person would lie under a bed, crying at three in the morning because someone else had gotten drunk? When I asked that question, everything I had heard about alcoholism became real. I was an alcoholic, and I could not stop drinking."

Ben vowed that he would do whatever was necessary to get well, and since that night, he has never had a single drink. He is an active member of Alcoholics Anonymous, and he and his wife work together in an alcoholism treatment program. "I used to promise my wife I'd never drink again," said Ben. "She heard enough promises to last a lifetime. Now I don't make promises. We both just live one day at a time, trusting in God's care."

A MERRY-GO-ROUND OF DENIAL

Ben had suffered serious public and personal consequences from his alcoholism for more than twenty years, and for twenty years he had successfully kept from himself the knowledge that he had a drinking problem. This merry-go-round of denial, far from being unusual, is one of the most typical and tragic aspects of alcoholism.

It is the rare alcoholic who recognizes that he has lost control of his drinking. "I knew I was an alcoholic," admitted one fifty-seven-year-old patient, "but I didn't see any way out. I gave up thinking my life could ever be different, and I tried to appear to my family and friends as if I wasn't addicted."

The majority of alcoholics are not pretending when they deny their addiction. Whatever hopeless awareness exists at a subconscious level, they often consciously believe that they are normal drinkers. The typical alcoholic can sit in a doctor's office drunk, with shaking hands, a swollen red nose, and an enlarged liver, and confidently claim to be a social drinker. One of my patients spent his mornings kneeling in front of a commode, vomiting up blood and intermittently drinking from a can of beer. As far as he was concerned, he didn't have a problem.

For some, denial takes more subtle forms. The compliant alcoholic may periodically admit to her family or friends that she is "a no-good drunk" and beg for help and understanding. Sometimes she promises never to drink again. Sometimes she simply asks to be loved and accepted despite her human weakness. At such moments, the alcoholic is usually extremely persuasive, but in all likelihood, she has no genuine understanding of her addiction and no intention of giving up drinking. Her motivation, however unconscious, is to capture the sympathy of her audience and to discourage any effort to interfere with her drinking.

I can quit when I want. I don't drink as much as Beth. I'll stop next year. These are the standard delusions of the alcoholic, and the longer she drinks, the more pronounced her denial becomes. It is not unusual for a person lying in a hospital bed, dying of alcohol-induced cirrhosis, to assert confidently that she has never had even so much as a single drink.

How can the alcoholic ignore the obvious consequences of his drinking and repeatedly deny his addiction? The full answer to this perplexing question is not yet known, but it is possible to identify some important contributing factors.

8

The Supporting Cast

~

However strong our personal commitment to honesty and integrity, all human beings suffer from some degree of self-deception. We often delay facing unpleasant truths about ourselves as long as possible and may refuse to admit even our most obvious weaknesses.

Frequently, honest self-assessment begins only *after* we have paid a substantial price for our delusion. When the painful consequences of our actions outweigh the pleasure they bring us, we suddenly find ourselves giving serious thought to changing our behavior.

Patients suffering from high blood pressure are a case in point. High blood pressure, or hypertension, is a serious, life-threatening disease. It is also usually painless. Because patients with high blood pressure seldom feel sick, they commonly ignore their doctor's repeated warnings about diet, exercise, and proper medications. It is often only when they suffer painful consequences—a heart attack, stroke, severe headaches, kidney failure, or partial blindness—that they take seriously their doctor's advice. Unfortunately, by then the damage is often irreparable.

Alcoholics behave in much the same way. They suffer from an

overpowering craving for alcohol and the firm conviction that they cannot live without drinking. The longer their addiction continues, the stronger their craving becomes and the fewer resources they possess for resisting temptation. Unless the painful consequences of drinking *clearly* outweigh its known benefits, the alcoholic is unlikely to surrender his or her right to drink.

As miserable as most alcoholics may seem, in most cases they are not miserable enough, fast enough. Alcoholics are sheltered from some of the most disturbing and painful results of their drinking by (a) the chemical effects of alcohol on their judgment and memory; (b) their sophisticated system of psychological defense mechanisms; and (c) the well-intentioned efforts of the people closest to them.

CHEMICAL DAMAGE TO JUDGMENT AND MEMORY

The toxic effects of alcohol seriously impair the alcoholic's ability to judge the appropriateness of his actions. With inhibitions removed and mood temporarily elevated, the alcoholic can interpret even his most embarrassing and harmful actions as episodes of special insight and social success. Since drunkenness is often one of the few remaining pleasures in his life, the alcoholic may recall his intoxicated moments in a rosy, bucolic light. This *euphoric recall* conceals from the alcoholic the true nature of his behavior, and he is often surprised to discover that relationships have been permanently damaged by actions he remembers as unusually witty or clever.

The alcoholic's ability to learn from his mistakes is further damaged by chemically induced memory blackouts. As we saw in Ben's story, some of the alcoholic's most shocking and reprehensible actions leave no memory trace on his brain. "He acts as if nothing happened," said the confused wife of an alcoholic after a nightmarish evening of fighting. "Am I making the whole thing up?" Often, from the alcoholic's perspective, nothing did happen. While the alcoholic's spouse is left to doubt her sanity and to cope with searing memories of verbal and/or physical abuse, the alcoholic is cut off from vital feedback about his behavior by the chemical impairment of his memory. He has nothing to forget because there is nothing he remembers.

REPRESSION

In every life there are some events too painful or shameful to dwell on for long. "If a fifty-year-old man could and did remember in a single moment *all* his shameful and painful acts in a half-century of living, he would go into an irreversible emotional collapse," said Dr. Vernon Johnson. "He simply could not bear such a burden—it would turn him into a gibbering idiot."[1]

In an attempt to live with the burden of past mistakes and wrongdoing, even the healthiest of human beings repress difficult memories. *Repression* is the act of burying past events and actions so deeply that they are removed from conscious thought. This burial is an *automatic defense mechanism* of the wounded human psyche, and as such it almost always takes place without conscious awareness.

For the alcoholic, repression is a full-time job. To preserve her shaky self-esteem and her right to drink, the alcoholic must distance herself from her own humiliating and perhaps immoral actions. She represses painful memories deep in her subconscious, where she hopes they will do no further harm. In reality they fuel her self-hatred and increase her need for alcohol. An alcoholic can become so adept at repression that she can convince herself in minutes that she did not say or do the things from which she still suffers obvious consequences.

ENABLING

Afflicted by memory distortions and armed with well-developed defense mechanisms, the alcoholic is trapped in a cage that has few openings from the outside. He seldom spontaneously recognizes his addiction, and he is dependent upon others to help him escape his delusion. At the same time, as we will see in Chapters 17–18, the sooner the alcoholic's circle of supporters intervene, the more likely it is that the alcoholic will recover.

Sadly, the people closest to the alcoholic, acting out of their own good intentions, fears, dependency, and emotional wounds, often become the supporting cast for the alcoholic's addiction. They may inadvertently enable the alcoholic to continue drinking by accepting his distorted version of reality and sheltering him from the painful consequences of his conduct. This common dynamic, called *enabling*, is rooted at least partly in our instinct to comfort and protect sick people. For the alcoholic, whose most important lifeline to sobriety is honest self-assessment, it has disastrous consequences.

THE MISSED DIAGNOSIS

Several years ago, a patient of mine who had consulted numerous doctors and specialists was diagnosed with depression. She was admitted to an inpatient psychiatric program, where she spent a seemingly profitable three months. The day she was released, she was walking out the door when a staff member came running after her. "Wait, we may have missed your diagnosis. You might be suffering from alcoholism!" She was indeed an alcoholic, and after attending Alcoholics Anonymous and an outpatient treatment program, she has been sober for more than twenty years.

Almost every alcoholic has a similar story to tell. The average alcoholic visits her doctor several times a year, complaining of headaches, depression, night sweats, high blood pressure, diarrhea, and marriage problems. Rarely, if ever, does she complain of alcoholism. Her goal, perhaps unconscious, is to conceal her addiction and get treatment for her symptoms so that she can continue drinking without physical pain.

Despite significant advances in equipping medical students with tools for early diagnosis of substance abuse and medical intervention,[2] a large number of doctors still inadvertently cooperate with the alcoholic's denial. Many recognize only the late-stage symptoms of addiction and do not routinely give a screening test for addiction. When confronted with the vague physical and psychological complaints of the alcoholic, these doctors may respond by writing a prescription for tranquilizers or other mood-altering drugs.

With this simple gesture, every year thousands of doctors help perpetuate the addiction of their alcoholic patients. Mood-altering drugs easily substitute for one another and may only further distort the alcoholic's already muddled perceptions. Like a good stiff drink, drugs may enable the alcoholic to satisfy his craving and cope with the anxiety produced by addiction. "My doctor gave me sleeping pills, tranquilizers, and antidepressants," remembered Ben. "Who needs alcohol with a deal like that?"

Because mood-altering drugs are interchangeable, an individual addicted to one drug, such as alcohol, easily becomes "cross-addicted" to another. Cross-addicted alcoholics have a substantially lower recovery rate than alcoholics in general, and they are more likely to die from an accidental overdose or suffer irreparable brain damage. It is important to note that mood-altering pills and alcohol are a potentially lethal combination for anyone, not just the alcoholic. Teenagers in particular need to be warned that drugs and alcohol, when taken together, have a *synergistic* effect—the total impact of their mix is greater than the sum of their parts.

"NOT IN MY FAITH GROUP!"

Joan was an active member of her synagogue and served on the board of a number of nonprofit organizations. When her teenage children entered a rebellious stage and her husband's work kept him out late at night, she began to drink an occasional nightcap. Within three years of her first drink, Joan was downing a quart of Jack Daniels a day. For five years she drank compulsively, experienced blackouts, carried on violent arguments with her husband—and never missed a Sabbath observance. The support she found in her religious community enabled her to survive emotionally from one week to the next and, despite many intimate discussions, no one in her synagogue knew that Joan was addicted to alcohol. Her friends accepted her explanation that she was depressed and only learned of Joan's alcoholism after she was recovering.

Perhaps you are saying, "It couldn't happen in *our* synagogue [or church or temple or mosque]." It can happen in any faith group, but it is the rare faith community that knows the extent of its drinking problem. Because people of faith often fail to distinguish between drunkenness and addiction, and because alcoholics may be viewed in a judgmental and moralistic light, many faith groups mistakenly believe that their fellow believers are immune from the danger of addiction. This conviction allows them to overlook even the most obvious symptoms of alcoholism, particularly if they appear in a religious leader.

An alcoholic coming from a faith background is likely to share the judgmental attitude of his fellow believers, and though he denies his addiction, he is secretly convinced that God has permanently rejected him. His own behavior may appall him. When he repeatedly drinks too much, and emotionally or even physically abuses his family and friends, he is violating not just social codes but his own spiritual principles. The dissonance between belief and action is even more pronounced in alcoholic religious leaders, who may participate in all kinds of uncontrolled behavior but must still give moral and spiritual leadership to their congregations.

In my own faith tradition, Christian alcoholics are sometimes dismissed as hypocrites, but the disgrace and guilt they feel are far removed from the arrogant complacency condemned by Jesus. At the same time, the spiritual anguish of the alcoholic is seldom redemptive. He may have repented of drinking more times than he can remember, but because he cannot imagine life without alcohol, his remorse never leads to a changed life. His spiritual beliefs only increase his sense of condemnation and compel him to adopt increasingly extreme denial measures.

SPIRITUAL ENABLING

Alcoholics may visit their pastor, rabbi, or religious leaders to complain of marriage problems, financial difficulties, or depression. If these leaders have not been educated about substance abuse, they are unlikely to ask the kinds of questions that would surface the underlying problem of addiction. Since his addiction remains concealed, the alcoholic is allowed to ventilate his feelings, and he and his family may learn practical tips for weathering their domestic crises without addressing his alcoholism. Pressures that might otherwise force the alcoholic to admit his addiction are effectively reduced. The alcoholic may become emotionally dependent upon his pastor or counselors, and this umbrella of external authority may further reduce his sense of responsibility for his own actions.

"ON THE JOB, HE'S NOT A BAD FELLOW."

Dr. Joseph Cruse wrecked his automobile while driving under the influence of alcohol. As a professional courtesy, his emergency room doctor "lost" the results of his blood-alcohol test. For the next eleven years and through six hospital admissions, Dr. Cruse's colleagues ignored his intoxicated behavior and falsified his medical records. On his sixth admission to the hospital, a self-inflicted stab wound from a suicide attempt was labeled "an accidental cut."

"They covered up for me because I'm a buddy—a colleague," recalled Dr. Cruse, a recovering alcoholic and former medical director of the Betty Ford Center for alcohol and drug addiction. "They did it with the best of intentions. But if they hadn't covered it up the first time, when I had the auto accident, somebody possibly could have saved me and my family eleven years of unhappiness."[3]

Conservative estimates place the number of heavy drinkers in the United States at 6 percent of the workforce. These men and women cost their employers and business associates billions of dollars a year, and they are responsible for a tragic number of work-related accidents. Despite their high turnover rates, declining productivity, and the ever-present threat of a serious mishap, alcoholic employees are often kept on the job by their employers or fellow workers who tolerate or cover up for their addiction.

What accounts for this almost universal effort to protect the alcoholic employee? At one time or another, most of us have had a colleague who was addicted to alcohol, and we understand from our personal experience how complicated and paralyzing these situations can be. Many alcoholics are bright, capable people who, even functioning at half speed, are more qualified than their peers. By the time their addiction surfaces, they often have worked at their jobs for years and have established close friendships and personal ties with their fellow workers. These friends are not immune from the alcoholic's skill at rationalization and projection, nor do they wish to see him and his family lose their source of income.

The alcoholic's colleagues often help him keep his job at significant personal cost to themselves. They work extra hard to make up for his low productivity, cover up for his absences, and pick up the pieces after his most serious mistakes. These well-meaning efforts enable the alcoholic to continue drinking without paying the price of unemployment. His dependency may be increased until he is little more than a child dressed up in adult clothes. Finally his addiction progresses to such unmanageable stages that his employer may be forced to let him go.

Enablers on the job interfere with one of the single most motivating factors for recovery from addiction: the fear of being fired. Alcoholics who are guaranteed their jobs whether they drink or not, will drink. Those who are threatened with dismissal unless they complete treatment programs have one of the highest recovery rates of any group of addicted drinkers.

On the job, among friends, in the doctor's office, and in communities of faith, the alcoholic encounters a wealth of community support for his addiction. It is among family members, however, where the alcoholic finds his most faithful enablers. Here, the people who suffer most from his behavior become the people who inadvertently support his addiction. These enabling relationships, which develop as coping mechanisms for fear and helplessness, often follow a predictable pattern and cause alcoholism to be labeled by some mental health experts as "the family disease."

ALCOHOLISM IN THE WORKPLACE: SYMPTOMS CHECKLIST

- Failure to show up on Monday morning

- Erratic behavior and unexplained outbursts of anger

- Depression

- Unkempt appearance

- Smell of alcohol on the breath

- Tremors

- Family stress

- Frequent job changes

9

A Partner's Point of View

⁀

Belinda was a loyal wife. When her husband, Ben, whose story was told in Chapter 7, was thrown in jail for public drunkenness, she bailed him out. She cleaned up after him when he was sick, put him to bed when he passed out, and made up stories to tell his colleagues when he failed to show up for work on Monday. Although she was painfully embarrassed when Ben arrived drunk at their son's baseball game, she never allowed her children to complain about their father.

When Ben's binges became more frequent, Belinda turned to a friend for advice. "Find out what you're doing to make him drink," the man advised. "If you treat Ben right, he'll settle down."

Belinda stepped up her efforts to be a good wife. She fixed Ben's favorite foods and wore clothes that he liked. She tried not to bother him about household chores or finances.

At times Ben went for months without drinking. Then, just as Belinda began to believe his claims that he was permanently on the wagon, he would come home drunk. Belinda often resolved to take the kids and leave, but Ben always sobered up just before she packed her bags. After his binges, he was unusually kind and thoughtful.

Despite her better judgment, Belinda felt a renewal of hope. Maybe this time Ben really meant it when he said he wouldn't drink again.

As Ben's drinking escalated, his family began to suffer genuine hardship. There were unpaid bills, canceled vacations, and even cuts in the food budget. Occasionally there were embarrassing public scenes, but far worse was the constant fear that Ben would seriously hurt himself or someone else.

Belinda began to have chronic headaches and high blood pressure. Some days she was too depressed to get out of bed in the morning. She had little emotional energy for her children, and she felt increasingly tense and angry. "Ben's outlet was drinking; mine was yelling," she remembers. "My voice grew tight and shrill, and I was always finding fault with someone or something. When I saw dark circles under my eyes, I blamed Ben for making me into an ugly, hateful person. But deep down, I knew that if I could only be a better partner, Ben would stop drinking."

Belinda's profound sense of guilt and failure led to suicidal despair, and in desperation she began attending Al-Anon. Here she learned that she was not alone; there were millions of people who were married to alcoholics and felt and behaved just as she did. "It was such a relief to hear that I didn't *cause* Ben's drinking, I couldn't *control* it, and I couldn't *cure* it," remembered Belinda. "But it was months before I was willing to face my own shortcomings. I was so used to blaming everything on Ben that my spiritual maturity had come to a standstill."

Belinda still remembers the night she was finally able to let go. "Ben was late, and I was praying at the window. Usually I prayed with one eye shut and one eye open, telling God what to do. This time I told God that whatever happened, it would be okay. At that moment, the burden I had been carrying for years left me, and I went to fix dinner for the children."

Ben called late that evening. He had been arrested and needed

Belinda to post bail. Belinda told Ben how much she loved him. "For the first time in years, I really meant it," she recalled. She also told Ben that she would not be coming to bail him out. She was sorry he had gotten himself into a mess, but now he would have to get himself out.

It was the beginning of a new way of life in Belinda's family. She began spending more time with the children, and they could no longer tell simply by looking at her face whether or not their father was drinking. Belinda and the children began talking together about their relationships with one another and their hopes and dreams for the future.

Now when Ben came home drunk, Belinda greeted him without accusation and left him alone to deal with the consequences of his drinking. If he was sick, he cleaned himself up. If he passed out at night on the floor, he found himself in the same spot in the morning. When he was in an accident, he called the tow truck, paid the damages, and made his own explanations to the children and neighbors.

One night Ben returned home drunk and cried and begged Belinda to become the wife he once knew. For the first time in fourteen years, Belinda was unmoved by his tears. "You know where to get help," she told him. "When you're sick and tired of drinking, I know you'll go find it."

Within a year Ben was "sick and tired." The price of intoxication had been raised to painful levels, and he was no longer willing to live with the consequences of his addiction. He entered a treatment program and began a new life without alcohol.

For Belinda, Ben's sobriety was just one ingredient in the slow but steady recovery of their family. During twenty years of living with an alcoholic, the family had organized itself around addiction and had cut itself off from the outside world. They had come to believe that all their problems were consequences of their father's alcoholism, and their own personal growth had come to a standstill. Now, as individuals and a family unit, they were ready to begin the challenging, sometimes painful, but deeply rewarding process of healing from their own psychological and spiritual wounds.

10

The Family Trap

⌁

Alcoholism is a family affair. If we conservatively estimate that every alcoholic deeply affects at least four people, in the United States alone eighty million adults and children are spending a significant portion of their life energies trying to cope with the unpredictable and destructive behavior of an alcoholic.

On the surface, every alcoholic's family has a different story to tell. Some live with a "quiet drunk" who so passively drinks his life away that his family suffers from nothing except his absence. Some live with a "happy drunk," whose congenial nature makes it difficult for family members to take his addiction seriously. Still others must cope with a violent, sadistic alcoholic who terrorizes his family psychologically and/or physically. Alcoholism is the single greatest cause of domestic violence in the United States, and for these abused families, life becomes a periodic or daily nightmare unimaginable to more healthy families.

Whatever personality differences exist among alcoholics, their family members frequently react in predictable ways to the strain and confusion of living with an addict. These reactions may become as obsessive and compulsive as the alcoholic's own behavior, leaving family members feeling equally trapped and helpless.

THE PUZZLE OF FAMILY DENIAL

One of the most baffling aspects of alcoholism is the inability of the people closest to the alcoholic to recognize the reality of her addiction. It is thought that the average family with an alcoholic member waits seven years after the evidence of addiction is indisputable to admit that there is an alcoholic in the house. They are then likely to wait at least another two years before seeking help. Some family members and friends continue to deny the alcoholic's addiction long after he or she has died from an alcohol-related disease or accident.

PERSISTENT DENIAL

Recently a good friend of mine died of alcoholism at the age of forty-three. Doctors found her physical disabilities indicated she had been an alcoholic for a great many years. Yet six months before she died, her father told me impatiently that she wasn't an alcoholic, and named a dozen women who drank more and behaved far worse. All her friends and relations had assured her that she wasn't an alcoholic. Most of them still think she died of heart failure, a falsehood that the newspapers faithfully recorded.[1]

—JOHN BOIT MORSE

This persistent denial by family members and close friends, however senseless it may seem, has a peculiar logic of its own. In the early stages of addiction, there are seldom visible clues to distinguish an alcoholic from a heavy or even moderate drinker. When early warning signs do appear—increased consumption, frequent intoxication, personality change—the people closest to the alcoholic may be blinded by personal loyalties and the social stigma attached to alcoholism. For all of us, it is easier to believe that disturbing drinking patterns are normal behavior than to entertain the possibility that someone we know and love has developed a socially unacceptable addiction.

By the time an alcoholic is unquestionably addicted, his family and any remaining friends are usually caught up in the net of his sickness and often lose the ability to make an objective judgment about his condition. Several important factors contribute to the family's distorted perceptions:

ISOLATION

It is the rare family that talks together about the presence of an alcoholic in their midst. Shame and embarrassment build a wall of silence around each individual member and gradually cut off all but superficial communication. To make matters worse, the alcoholic may be remarkably skilled at playing one member of the family against another. One of my patients so effectively created division among her adult children that they completely stopped talking to one another. Her manipulative behavior aggravated normal wounds and resentments and effectively prevented any united effort to address her addiction. Family members often increase their isolation by gradually separating themselves from outside friends and interests. Children of alcoholics learn from painful experience not to invite friends home and may have trouble forming deep relationships with people outside their family. If they make friends, it is often only with other children of alcoholics.

The world of the alcoholic's family members often gradually narrows until it includes little more than the addicted drinker and those who circle in her orbit. This creates an increasingly comfortable drinking environment for the alcoholic and may force the family to be emotionally dependent upon her for their own sense of well-being.

EMOTIONAL DISTRESS

Sooner or later family members are likely to become trapped in much the same emotional turmoil that afflicts the alcoholic. They may feel guilty for "causing" the alcoholic to drink and for hating or resenting someone they know they should love. They are ashamed and embarrassed by the alcoholic's actions, and they are angry at their own helplessness. Fear of the alcoholic's unpredictable behavior mixes with vague anxieties about the future, and increasing isolation leads to loneliness and depression.

Family members of alcoholics seldom share their distressing feelings with others. Instead, they often ignore or suppress them and allow them to fester into despair and self-hatred. These feelings make it even more difficult for families to address the problems created by the addicted drinker.

THE CENTRICITY OF THE ALCOHOLIC

In a reasonably functional family, no one person is always center stage. Attention is given to the needs and talents of each member, and there is a healthy give-and-take between spouses, parents, and children.

In a family suffering from alcoholism, more often than not the alcoholic is the primary focus of everyone's attention. Because his behavior is unpredictable, he is the X-factor, and all thoughts automatically focus on him. What kind of mood is *he* in today? If he's sober, what will we do to keep *him* happy? If he's drunk, how will we pacify *him* or take care of *him*? How will we stay out of *his* way? The family is always on guard, trying to predict the unpredictable and hoping to keep a bad situation from becoming worse.

Because the family is isolated and in emotional turmoil, and because the alcoholic is the focus of their energies, it is easy for family members to adopt the alcoholic's perspective on reality. It is not that the alcoholic drinks too much, but that a spouse is irritating, the children are noisy, parents are unfair, or colleagues are incompetent. Family members internalize the rationalizations and projections of the alcoholic, and like the alcoholic, they can deny his addiction even while they are paying an extraordinary price for his drinking.

THE CHIEF ENABLER

Every member in the family of an alcoholic makes adjustments in his or her behavior to accommodate the alcoholic and shelter him from the consequences of his drinking. Usually, there is one person who stands out—*a chief enabler*. The chief enabler is commonly a spouse but can be a child or parent, a close friend or employer, or even a counselor or physician.

In the early years of addiction, the chief enabler may be motivated by love and concern for the alcoholic. She senses that he really can't control his drinking and tries to remove temptation by cutting off his supply of alcohol. She searches the house for hidden bottles, pours hundreds of dollars of liquor down the drain, dilutes his drinks, and tries to engineer his social life. She is irritated by friends who drink and "tempt" the alcoholic, and she stops accepting invitations to parties where alcohol is served.

Despite her efforts, the alcoholic continues to drink. In order to survive and reduce the pressures she believes are the cause of her spouse's addiction, the chief enabler picks up the responsibilities that the alcoholic lays down. She pays the bills, fixes the plumbing, and disciplines the children. She also lies to his boss about his absence from work, bails him out of jail, takes his side in drunk-driving accidents, and drives him to work when he loses his license. Frequently, she works longer hours or takes a second job to replace the income the alcoholic drinks away.

The good intentions of the chief enabler create for the alcoholic an increasingly comfortable environment in which to drink. His meals are cooked, his laundry done, even his transportation provided. The alcoholic neglects the responsibilities of adulthood, and in exchange, he receives the conveniences of life.

While the alcoholic is sheltered from the consequences of her addiction, the chief enabler experiences more and more failure. He cannot control his wife's drinking—or his own unpredictable emotions. He may become depressed, moody, irritable, and angry. He may nag and shout when he wants to be loving and kind. His disagreeable behavior aggravates his sense of guilt and shame, and his self-esteem declines. A discouraged patient recently told me, "I feel if I could just be a better husband, my wife would not drink so much."

The alcoholic often has an uncanny ability to play on human weaknesses. He or she may take advantage of a spouse's emotional turmoil and dependency and zero in on the points of greatest vulnerability, perhaps giving a devastating and partially accurate critique of character. And just when the nondrinking spouse has had enough, the alcoholic may sober up and be genuinely charming, the person the nondrinking partner intended to marry. These periods of sobriety may keep a husband or wife hanging on for years, hoping eventually to find the key to solving the partner's drinking problem.

Sooner or later, the chief enabler comes to the end of hope. Crying, begging, screaming, pleading, and praying have all failed. There are no more promises to be believed. In the absence of outside help, the chief enabler and other family members must now choose either to leave the alcoholic or to settle for a precarious détente.

COMPASSION—OR EMOTIONAL BONDAGE?

In my own faith tradition, I have found that many committed Christian women are particularly vulnerable to the emotional bondage generated by the alcoholic. They may be encouraged by church leaders to be patient and passive, to submit to their husband's authority, however abusive, and to "kill him with kindness." Unfortunately, for both the alcoholic and his wife, kindness is indeed the ultimate killer. In the absence of mature, adult love, the addicted drinker gets sicker, and his wife falls into a self-destructive pattern of living.

"Compassion," says the Reverend Joseph Kellerman, "is bearing with or suffering with a person, not suffering because of the unwillingness of the other person to suffer."[2] The suffering of a spouse of an alcoholic is seldom compassionate—or redemptive. It is a suffering often poisoned by self-pity and resentment. Genuine love is replaced by bitterness or martyrdom, or even a secret satisfaction in the alcoholic's childlike dependence on the chief enabler. The couple's relationship may become a macabre dance of sadism and masochism that threatens to destroy the integrity of both partners.

MOVING ON

Some spouses, parents, and children choose to leave the alcoholic. They are convinced that the addicted drinker is the source of all their problems, and that once he or she is left behind, they will be able to start a new and better life for themselves.

Studies show, however, that physical separation alone does not heal the wounds that come from living with an alcoholic. Children of alcoholics frequently marry alcoholics or become alcoholics themselves. The wives or husbands of alcoholics may say "never again" and marry a second alcoholic—or a third. They carry the seeds of failure with them: bitterness, resentment, guilt, low self-esteem, and anger. Sometimes, years after the alcoholic is gone, he or she is still the center of their fantasies for revenge and retribution.

A sad number of marriage partners and children choose to move on by killing themselves. The striking frequency of these desperate and final acts gives poignant testimony to the hopelessness that springs from living with an addicted drinker.

DÉTENTE

To an outside observer, it often seems bizarre that anyone would stay with a spouse who is an addict. From the inside, as always, the situation is much more complicated. There may be deep bonds of love and care that have survived years of addiction. A spouse, particularly if she is not working, may not have the financial resources to leave a bad relationship. Both partners may be locked in a dance of emotional dependence, and they may have grown accustomed to the high-energy mix of control and dependency that characterizes many alcoholic relationships. Spouses may be deeply frightened by the prospect of new relationships based on mutual respect.

Partners of alcoholics who cannot or will not desert their spouses may try to address the alcoholic's problem by changing doctors, friends, or even moving to a new city or neighborhood—the "geographic cure." None of these short-term solutions is likely to be effective, and eventually the nondrinking partner attempts to negotiate a détente. She does everything possible not to rock the boat, accommodating herself and the children to the alcoholic's drinking. The addicted drinker becomes the central organizing principle of family life, and family members direct most of their emotional energies toward a single goal—maintaining the status quo.

Unfortunately, the alcoholic's addiction refuses to stand still.

Alcoholic détente is a progressively unhealthy and interlocking system of relationships that impoverishes the lives of all members of the family, including the alcoholic. In this environment, the individuals most deeply hurt are the children. Caught between a paralyzed parent and an addicted parent, they become the unnoticed and untreated victims of alcoholism.

11

"Somebody's Going to Get It!"

~

Bella's father was a brilliant man with a photographic memory. Every day he read two or three books; every evening, he drank a fifth of Scotch.

On the job, Bella's father was quiet and reserved. At home, he was an unpredictable tyrant who physically abused his wife and emotionally terrorized his children. He had an odd habit of sitting and staring at Bella while she did her homework. Occasionally he put his hand on her head and left it there. "He was like a black hole," Bella remembered. "Sometimes when he looked at me, I ran upstairs and threw up."

Nights were difficult. More than once, Bella's father fell asleep with a burning cigarette in his hand and set fire to the living room carpet. One night he wandered into her room completely undressed and lay down on top of her. He passed out almost immediately, but Bella stayed awake until morning, trying not to move.

Bella never talked to anyone about her father's strange behavior, but she did everything she could to help her mother. She took responsibility for household chores and cooked the evening meal. At school, she was a model student who worked hard for her teachers' approval.

While Bella was still in grade school, her father's drinking escalated. He still reported to work every morning, but his behavior at home was increasingly sinister. The suicidal notes he left lying around the house took on a homicidal ring: "Somebody's going to get it," he threatened. Bella's mother divided the family shotgun into three parts and gave each of her children a segment to hide between his or her mattress.

One evening, when Bella was fourteen, her father fell and hit his head on a coffee table. After he stood up, he seemed unusually disoriented and angry. He followed Bella around as she put away the dinner dishes, staring at her with bloodshot, watery eyes. Bella was suddenly overwhelmed by her father's appearance, and she ran upstairs to her bedroom. In her fright she forgot her nightly responsibility of locking the front door. A few hours later, her father wandered outside and walked in front of an oncoming car. He was killed instantly.

Within a year of her father's death, Bella had blossomed academically and socially. Despite her many friendships, she never told anyone about her father or the responsibility she felt for his death. "When you're in your teens, it's almost impossible to find someone who can relate to the pain of growing up in an alcoholic home," said Bella. "A normal high-school girl is worried about her fingernails and guys. I knew there was no point in talking about my family's experience."

During college, Bella spent hours counseling troubled friends and was always willing to type a term paper or bake brownies for late-night study breaks. Her fellow students were attracted by her unselfish giving and genuine compassion. "Bella is always there when you need her," said more than one friend.

When Bella was in her early twenties, her eyesight began to fail. She wore thick glasses and more than once fainted on her way home from class. She often threw up after her evening meal and experienced crippling anxiety attacks. She began to stay alone in her room, rocking back and forth, hugging her knees and staring vacantly out the window. "What happened to Bella?" her friends asked in dismay. "She's the last person we expected to go off the deep end!"

Bella's "deep end" lasted for two years. She went from doctor to doctor looking for help, until she finally found a therapist who understood the unique needs of adult children of alcoholics. With his assistance, she was able to face her past and begin the healing process.

"My nervous breakdown was the most painful period of my life," recalled Bella. "But it was a gift from God. The defense mechanisms of my childhood—compulsive giving and excessive responsibility—were remarkably strong. They had served me well for years, enabling me to withstand the stress of my father's alcoholic behavior.

"As a teenager and young adult, my defensive behavior was re-inforced by my friends' approval. I spiritualized my wounds and convinced myself that compulsive giving and frenetic activity were signs of maturity. The truth is that I grew up with a wounded personality, and my relationships took the same form. Only the most painful of experiences could break through my defensive, compulsive behavior and expose it for what it really was: a crippling barrier to true spirituality and genuine love."

Today, Bella is still an unusually empathetic and giving person. She has a special sensitivity to people living on the margins of society and is usually willing to lend a hand in time of trouble. "The difference is that now I don't try to control everything and fix everyone," said Bella. "I let people take responsibility for their own pain. I'm no longer so eager to please or so quick to blame myself for other people's inappropriate behavior."

Bella is one of an estimated forty million children of alcoholics who have grown up, or are growing up, in the shadow of an unpredictable and often self-centered parent. Not all of these children have had a childhood as horrifying as Bella's—some are much better, some far worse—but few children in an alcoholic home grow up unwounded. These wounds can begin before birth, and almost always cast a long shadow into adulthood.

ALCOHOLISM AND SEXUAL ABUSE

Perhaps because of alcohol's effect on judgment and inhibition, alcohol abuse and addiction play a large role in the sexual abuse of children. The extent of emotional damage a child suffers is related to whether or not there is physical abuse in the home, and girls who have experienced both alcoholism and sexual abuse appear to suffer more deeply than any other group of abused children.[1]

12

Too Much Too Soon

~

Aida was pregnant for the first time. She was a heavy smoker and drinker, but she was very concerned about the health of her unborn child. During her first prenatal checkup, her doctor explained the serious consequences of substance abuse during pregnancy. Aida went home and temporarily gave up cigarettes and alcohol, but within two weeks she was smoking again and drinking a bottle of wine a day. In seven months, she gave birth to a six-pound baby boy suffering from irreversible brain damage. He was one of three thousand babies born each year with serious alcohol-related birth defects.

When a pregnant woman drinks alcoholically or heavily, there is a significant risk that her baby will be born with *fetal alcohol syndrome.* This disturbing cluster of birth defects includes mental retardation, stunted growth, and odd facial deformities. Fetal alcohol syndrome is the number three cause of birth defects associated with brain damage, and a staggering 10 percent of alcohol-related health-care funds are spent caring for these victims.[1] No one knows how many more unborn children suffer indirectly from maternal drinking because of falls, fights, and malnutrition.

Men who drink heavily and/or addictively may also threaten the health and lives of their unborn children. Murder is the number one cause of death for pregnant women, and the abuse of alcohol and drugs plays a role in the majority of these deaths.

ALCOHOL AND PREGNANCY

No one knows how much alcohol a pregnant woman must drink to harm an unborn child. Alcohol crosses the placenta freely, is rapidly absorbed into a baby's bloodstream, and is slowly metabolized by a liver not yet fully developed. The result is that even small amounts of alcohol (a half ounce) can affect the breathing movements of a child in utero. Moderate daily amounts of alcohol (one ounce) have been shown to dramatically reduce a child's birth weight.

All women of childbearing age must keep in mind that there is no known "safe" amount of alcohol a pregnant woman can drink. This is especially true in the first seven weeks of pregnancy, when women are often unaware that they are carrying a child.

THE DEVELOPING CHILD

Derek is worried; his mother drinks too much. After school and in the summer, Derek takes care of his younger brother and sisters. His brother, four, is a chronic troublemaker. His twin sisters, age five, live in a world of their own. One cries easily and hides in a closet at the first sign of trouble; the other laughs and acts silly, even when everyone else is sad. Derek tries to make his brother and sisters behave so their mother won't drink, but usually they don't listen. They call Derek bossy and refuse to do their chores.

Derek works hard to fix things for his family. He does the laundry, sweeps the floor, gives baths, and mows the lawn. When his mother comes home drunk, he puts her to bed. If one of the younger children is sick, he stays home from school. But no matter how hard Derek works, he always feels anxious and afraid. Things are falling apart faster than he can put them together.

Derek is eleven years old. He is one of an estimated six million children and teenagers currently living with an alcoholic parent.[2] (An unknown number live with two alcoholic parents.) Like most of these boys and girls, Derek is growing up too quickly in a home environment devoid of the most important ingredients of a healthy childhood: love, limits, and consistency.

Few alcoholics are capable of the sustained effort necessary for communicating parental love to their children. "You showed affection only when drunk," wrote one adult child to her alcoholic father. "And that kind of affection is meaningful only to another drunk person. We could be your good buddies then, and yet we hated ourselves for doing so because we knew it was just the booze talking."[3]

In many homes with an alcoholic parent, there is no talking at all. Meal times are silent affairs—or shouting matches. If children attempt to carry on a conversation with a parent, the result is often a painful monologue. "When you come home from school, and something really good or bad happened that day, you want to tell someone," said a ten-year-old child of an alcoholic. "But no one wants to listen. It's better not to get happy or sad. It's better not to feel things."

EMOTIONAL DISTRESS

Even while children growing up in an alcoholic home attempt to shut off their normal emotions, they are often caught up in a whirlpool of shame, embarrassment, fear, and guilt. They instinctively look up to their parents and want to admire them, but they are repelled by their alcoholic behavior. Children feel deeply responsible for their parents' drinking but are acutely aware of their own help-lessness. Their welfare is tied to the behavior of an unpredictable person, and they cannot make the drinking go away, no matter how hard they try.

The chronic anxiety of children of alcoholics is aggravated by the mixed signals they may receive from both parents. Discipline is often sporadic, at best. When alcoholics are drunk, they may be unusually loving, totally oblivious, or exceptionally brutal. When they sober up, guilt and shame may cause a swing in the other direction. They may become extremely permissive or tyrannically strict, reversing decisions that they made while drunk. Whichever way the pendulum swings, growing children soon learn that there is only one established boundary in their lives—the mood of their alcoholic parent.

ALCOHOLISM AND PHYSICAL ABUSE

The moral decline of addicted drinkers can result in the physical abuse of children. Each year in the United States alone, three million children are referred to child protection services, and between fifteen hundred and two thousand are killed. Drinking parents are involved in the majority of child abuse cases.

These statistics, however heartrending, cannot adequately communicate the terror of a defenseless child who, year after year, is physically and psychologically tormented by a violent and unpredictable parent. For many of these children, survival becomes a full-time job, and their nightmare ends only when they are driven to suicide or murder.

MORAL DILEMMA

This parental inconsistency is particularly damaging to a child's moral development. Children learn the difference between right and wrong primarily in the home, and they are easily confused if parents preach one message and practice another. Frequently in alcoholic homes, both parents follow a double standard as their behavior declines to meet the demands of addiction.

One common difficulty for children of alcoholics is honesty. Taught at an early age to tell the truth, they may then hear their father lie about his drinking, and their mother lie to cover it up. They themselves may be asked to tell "white lies" to protect the family's reputation. As a result, some children report that they struggle with the problem of compulsive lying long after they have committed themselves to being honest adults.

"For most of my life, I lied about things that didn't matter at all," said one adult child of an alcoholic. "I found myself saying preposterous things, and then I was too embarrassed to retract them. Over the years, I lost many friends because they learned I could not be trusted.

"The turning point came when I met a man who remained my friend even after he discovered that I didn't always tell the truth. His acceptance and loving confrontation enabled me to face my problem honestly. I realized that just as my father was addicted to alcohol, I was addicted to lying. Through much counseling and hard work, I learned as an adult what most people learn as children—how to tell the truth."

THE PARALYSIS OF THE NONDRINKING PARENT

Whatever level of abuse or neglect develops in an alcoholic home, when problems first begin, young children automatically turn to their nondrinking parent for emotional and spiritual support. Only a few find it. In some families, the nondrinking parent is able to put aside his or her own pain and focus attention on the critical needs of a child growing up in a crisis-oriented environment.

More commonly, however, the wife or husband of an alcoholic is too exhausted by the day-to-day trauma of living with an addicted spouse to give even normal amounts of attention to children, much less the extra parenting needed. The love they mean to demonstrate comes wrapped in a garment of fatigue and chronic irritation. Their pre-occupation and frustration signal to a child that he or she is unloved and unwanted, and instead of becoming allies in a difficult situation, children and parents may become increasingly burdensome to one another.

Frequently, children of alcoholics feel angrier at their nondrinking parent than at the alcoholic. They may sympathize with the alcoholic as a weak or sick person, but they see their nondrinking mother or father as a powerful adult who could put a stop to the family's problems if he or she tried. The child may be further alienated by the rationalizations and accusations of the alcoholic, which become increasingly believable as the behavior of the nonalcoholic parent deteriorates. The child may come to blame the nonalcoholic parent for all the family's problems, including the alcoholic's drinking.

A CRISIS OF CONFIDENCE

With one parent unpredictable and the other emotionally para-lyzed, children of an alcoholic quickly learn that they cannot depend on their parents to meet their basic needs. This is a devastating vac-uum in the life of a dependent child. Children learn the art of trust-ing others by first trusting their parents. If they are forced to surrender their natural dependency prematurely, they may become deeply sus-picious and mistrustful of their fellow human beings. While a certain amount of skepticism is necessary and prudent, the inability to estab-lish relationships based on mutual trust is a paralyzing emotional handicap. It is a legacy that effectively isolates children of alcoholics from the deep friendships and commitments necessary for healthy personality development.

Children who cannot rely on their parents are forced to rely on themselves. Unfortunately for children of alcoholics, their external and internal resources are substantially more limited than those of even ordinary children. They have poor role models for handling stress and crises, and little experience with spontaneous, flexible behavior. They often are left to guess which parental behaviors are considered normal human responses, and they may have no one with whom they can talk over their confusion. This confusion is then aggravated by the whirl of their strong, unexpressed, and painful emotions.

Worst of all, such children often suffer from a critical deficiency in their self-esteem. Children learn to value themselves by experiencing loving approval and consistent discipline from their parents. What children of alcoholics often experience is constant criticism. They fall short of the perfectionism and unrealistic expectations of their addicted parent, and their fledgling sense of worth is undercut by a paralyzing sense of inadequacy. "I could never do enough to please my father," said one adult child of an alcoholic. "He was so demanding that we were forced to sweep all the stones in our driveway in the same direction. I grew up with tremendous fear of not producing, or being caught doing nothing."

Crippled by insecurity and still in the tender stages of personality development, children of alcoholics are often asked to handle increasingly difficult circumstances. The methods they use to survive—and children of alcoholics are survivors—reveal a great deal about the human personality and its remarkable capacity for coping with crises.

13

Games Children Play

A s the father of three and grandfather of eleven, I have learned that children do a lot of their growing up by trial and error. In a relatively healthy family environment, most children try out a variety of ways of responding to an unfamiliar world. Eventually, they discover what works for them and what doesn't. Ideally, they learn when it is best to take charge, when to give in, when to think for themselves, and when to defer to the opinions and needs of others. They make frequent miscalculations, but gradually they adjust their behavior to fit the changing nature of their environment and relationships.

For most children of alcoholics, this flexible maturation process is an unaffordable luxury. In order to cope with an unpredictable parent (or two), they may lock themselves into rigid roles within the family system very early in life. This defensive behavior, while it may appear healthy and appropriate, can become as compulsive and obsessive as the alcoholic's addiction.

The coping styles of children of alcoholics, of all ages, are on one level as diverse as human beings themselves. However, some basic patterns have emerged in the literature about adult children of alcoholics, and identifying these roles can be helpful in the recovery process.[1] The coping styles employed by children of alcoholics include:

- becoming unusually responsible
- compulsive helping or placating
- always adjusting or giving in
- causing trouble

Whether children adopt one role or a combination of roles, their defensive behavior usually serves them well for years. It compensates for parental inadequacies, covers the gaps in their emotional development, and brings a semblance of stability and order to otherwise chaotic lives. Because they have learned to trust its reliability, children carry their coping strategy into adulthood, where, under the strain of adult relationships and responsibilities, they may come face-to-face with the dark side of their developmental years.

THE RESPONSIBLE CHILD: A FAMILY HERO

In almost every disrupted family, there is one child, often the oldest, who takes on the duties of the missing or overburdened parent. Like Bella and Derek in Chapters 11 and 12, these responsible, adultlike children prepare meals, worry about finances, look out for the welfare of younger siblings, and try to keep the family functioning as normally as possible. Sometimes they play the role of counselor, settling disputes between their parents and trying to smooth over broken relationships. At times they play the part of "enabler," putting the alcoholic to bed, cleaning up after him when he is sick, and pouring out his liquor supply. I knew one teenage boy who regularly slept on the floor in front of his alcoholic mother's bedroom door to prevent her from falling down the stairs at night.

At school, the *family hero* is usually an overachiever. Such children may make above-average grades, run for class president, or become disciplined athletes. They work hard to accomplish difficult goals and win the approval of teachers and authority figures. Often they are gifted organizers or unusually adept at leading their classmates.

As overachieving children become adults, they commonly cover the gaps in their emotional development with hard work and self-discipline. Their inner drive to achieve may lead them into early professional success and to positions of leadership within their faith groups and communities. They are admired for "making good" in spite of a bad home life. Many, in fact, become doctors and nurses or enter other helping professions.

While outwardly these hardworking men and women appear self-confident and capable, their inner lives are marked by emotional turmoil. Reflected one adult child of an alcoholic, a minister, "I was always extremely tense. I had an inner drive to please people and the feeling that I never quite did. I dismissed compliments almost before I heard them, knowing that they surely sprang from misperceptions. I knew I had a gift for motivating and leading people, but I panicked if I wasn't in charge. Either I was calling the shots, or I felt like my whole world was crumbling."

The need to be in control *all the time* makes the family hero uncomfortable in relationships without an established hierarchy. She may avoid adult friendships (and the unpredictability they entail) and surround herself with people who can be controlled and manipulated. She may hold a desperate belief that every question must have an answer, and her rigid, black-and-white approach to problems often alienates her from other healthy adults, including her own family. As a result, she becomes increasingly lonely and depressed.

Despite emotional isolation, the family hero continues to accept more and more challenging responsibilities. When she finds herself surrounded by people and circumstances she can't control, her anxiety escalates. As a child, she learned to handle stress by working harder; now as an adult she is ignorant of the art of relaxation. She does not know how to let go, and she cannot share her anxieties with anyone. All she can do is work harder to control herself and other people. She may become increasingly inflexible and defensive, and take on bigger and more demanding projects. The greater her responsibilities, the more insecure she feels; and the more insecure she feels, the more responsibility she accepts. In this manner, the family hero may spend years compulsively feeding the very fire she is trying to extinguish.

THE PLACATER-HELPER

The *placater-helper* child lives his life in the orbit of other people's feelings. As a young child, he is unusually sensitive to the hurts and needs of his family members, and he tries hard to diminish their disappointments and fears. He is quick to pick up on signals: anger, hurt, resentment, sadness. He tries to smooth over conflicts before they develop and attempts to heal the hurts of others by giving of himself.

As the placater-helper enters adulthood, he is often surrounded by a host of needy people who are attracted to his unselfish giving and compassion. He is an empathic counselor and a listening ear, who seldom disagrees with anyone. He may apologize endlessly for events outside of his control: "I'm sorry your dinner is cold . . . I'm sorry you don't feel well . . . I'm sorry your boss is unfair." The placating child accepts responsibilities that others avoid, and no matter how busy he becomes, he seldom says no to a request for help.

The compulsive giving of the placater-helper cuts him off from the mutual give-and-take of adult relationships. He is convinced that the high regard of his friends depends on his ability to outgive others, and he is unable to receive love and concern for himself. He becomes ever more lonely and depressed but cannot share these feelings with anyone; all his relationships are built on the myth of his own indestructibility and lack of emotional needs.

In some disrupted families, the placating child is also the family clown. These unusually perceptive children have a knack for turning even the most awkward moments into a joke, and they learn to defuse anger or violence with well-placed humor. As they enter adulthood, family clowns may become compulsive talkers and may be unusually high-strung. But even in the most painful moments, they cover their deepest feelings with a joke. Only the most persistent and perceptive of friends can break through their cover of humor to address the wounds that lie beneath.

THE ADJUSTER

In the unpredictable environment of an alcoholic home, anything can happen. The *adjusting child* is always prepared—to do nothing. She is an adapter, a child so paralyzed by her own fears and sense of inadequacy that she no longer tries to initiate actions of her own. Instead, she opts for a relatively pain-free existence of "going with the flow." Accepting with a shrug the arbitrarily canceled vacation, the sudden fight, the unexpected slap, she recognizes that the only unchanging conditions of her life are her powerlessness and isolation. She often separates herself from her family and spends inordinate time alone in her room, creating a fantasy world.

At school and at church, the adjuster is a "lost child," the youngster whose name no one remembers, the boy or girl whose shy and apathetic presence seldom leaves more than a fleeting impression. In a room full of noisy children clamoring for attention, the adjusting child easily slips between the cracks—and is happy there. He or she prefers to be left alone, having learned that daydreams are safer and more satisfying than unpredictable human encounters.

As the adjuster enters adulthood, she seldom has a sense of direction and purpose. She continues to perceive herself as powerless, without choices or alternatives. She usually gravitates toward people who are as emotionally detached as she is, or she marries a spouse who re-creates the chaos of her childhood. In such marriages, the adjusting adult-child does what she knows best: she adapts. She becomes a passive spectator to the family's difficulties and is easily manipulated by people around her.

The emotional detachment and apathy of the adjusting child are often mistaken for serenity. Serenity may come when we accept the things we cannot change, but the adjusting child, sadly, accepts the fact that she cannot change anything—ever. As the years go by, this acceptance leads her further and further from the peace and tranquillity she seeks. She becomes trapped in loneliness and despair.

THE REBELLIOUS CHILD

In most disrupted families, there is at least one child whose name spells T-R-O-U-B-L-E. For this child, the rules are made to be broken. He thumbs his nose at authority—at home, at school, at church, and on the playground. He is so constantly in trouble that he soon draws attention away from the alcoholic. He is increasingly singled out as the source of the family's growing problems, and he may become the family scapegoat.

The rebellious child has discovered an important principle of child development: negative attention is better than no attention at all. His self-esteem is often even lower than that of his performance-oriented siblings. He roots his fragile sense of self in the awareness that he is "bad," and he gravitates toward friends who likewise have poor self-esteem. Often he runs with a "wild crowd" who instinctively head for trouble wherever it can be found.

Because drugs and alcohol are a common focus of teenage rebellion, the troubled child of an alcoholic is likely to experiment with, or abuse, addictive substances at an early age. Early use of alcohol is a risk factor for alcoholism, and combined with the strong possibility of an inherited predisposition for addiction, the rebellious child is more likely than not to be in serious trouble with drugs or alcohol, or both, before he has left adolescence. And regardless of whether or not he develops a full-fledged addiction, the rebellious child is at high risk for spending at least part of his adolescence behind bars or in psychiatric care.

The rebellious child enters adulthood with a chip on her shoulder and a penchant for making poor decisions. She may drop out of school, marry early or have illegitimate children, avoid job training, and run up debts she cannot pay. Her ability to survive in the adult world by legal means is seriously hampered by the shortsighted decisions of her youth, and she may feel increasingly powerless and insignificant. Her growing frustration may propel her in the direction of violent and illegal acts.

WHEN COPING STRATEGIES FAIL

Whether or not children of alcoholics become responsible, placating, adjusting, or rebellious, or try out a combination of these roles, sooner or later their coping strategies break down. The behavior that was a boon for them as a child becomes a burden to them as an adult, and they experience unexpected failure. They discover that not everyone can be manipulated, and those who can be will eventually react with anger and bitterness. They encounter people who will not be placated and situations to which they cannot adjust. Lies catch up with the compulsive liar, and the rebellious adult child may find that the price of adult delinquent behavior has been raised beyond that which he or she is willing to pay.

The breakdown of old roles and behavior patterns may take

decades, but when it happens, adult children of alcoholics feel suddenly bereft. The gaps in their emotional development are exposed, and old wounds demand their due. At this point, the adult child often enters a new period of crisis that may threaten his or her career, marriage, sanity—or life.

THE ADULT CRISIS

Annie was an intelligent and serious woman. She was also a high-school teacher, the mother of four grown children, and the wife of a likable, easygoing realtor. She worked hard, and while she sometimes resented her husband's lightheartedness and her own role as the family "heavy," she had been happily married for thirty years.

One Christmas, Annie's children uncorked an expensive bottle of wine. Annie was not a drinker—her childhood had been made miserable by an alcoholic father—but now with her own children grown, she felt more tolerant. She accepted one glass of wine, then a second. She was surprised how good two drinks made her feel. She felt relaxed and carefree, and for the first time in her married life, she understood her husband's jokes.

During the same holiday, over another bottle of wine, Annie and her oldest daughter had a long and intimate conversation. It had always been difficult for Annie to talk freely about her feelings. Now, drink in hand, she spoke candidly about her doubts and insecurities. Her daughter was sympathetic—and grateful. "I felt like I never knew you before," she said, giving her mother a rare hug. "It's like discovering a new and wonderful member of the family."

In the months that followed, Annie found that a glass of wine was a reliable method for relieving the pressures of a lifetime of difficult responsibilities. While drinking, she no longer felt as if she were missing some key to life that everyone else automatically possessed. Her friends and family responded warmly to "the new Annie," and it seemed to her that a heavy burden of isolation and anxiety had suddenly dropped from her shoulders.

Within ten years, however, Annie had a new burden. She was an alcoholic. To her own horror, she was drinking up to a bottle of wine a day. She made frequent resolutions to quit, but it seemed impossible to pass up a drink at dinner. Somehow one drink always led to another, and Annie spent her evenings sprawled in front of the television, too drunk to talk coherently. In the mornings, she woke up with a headache, hating herself and counting the hours until dinnertime.

Like Annie, most children of alcoholics grow up declaring, "It will never happen to me." They have seen firsthand the misery of addiction, and they are convinced that these grim experiences are adequate protection against marrying an alcoholic or becoming alcoholics themselves. They leave home thinking that their problems are behind them, and in comparison to the misery of their past, their future seems remarkably bright.

Unfortunately, many adult children of alcoholics carry their past with them, like a hidden but opportunistic illness. Although many children leave home as early as possible to escape the alcoholic, their risk of developing alcoholism remains three to four times that of children growing up without alcoholic parents.[2] A significant percentage also marry alcoholics. Many, like Annie, find out relatively late in life that alcohol serves as a quick chemical solution to the unresolved conflicts of their childhoods. With a drink, the family hero can relax, the placater can forget about other people's feelings, the adjuster feels more socially adept, and the troublemaker feels a new sense of power and self-confidence. Perhaps unaware that inheritance patterns place them at high risk for developing addiction, these men and women may quickly move from social to compulsive drinking. Before they or their families know what is happening, they develop an addiction to the chemical they have feared and hated all their lives.

Addiction and alcoholic marriages are only two of the threats facing adult children of alcoholics. In their twenties or early thirties, they may discover that their childhood defense mechanisms are falling apart under the combined pressures of marriage, children, and professional responsibilities. With few personal resources to fall back on, these men and women may find themselves acting in desperation and completely out of character. A young minister with three children collapses in the pulpit and later takes his own life. A well-known youth worker in a major metropolitan city, a gifted young woman to whom hundreds of teenagers look for guidance, becomes suddenly depressed and is institutionalized with a psychotic breakdown. A respected community leader runs off with a girl half his age, leaving his wife and children in a financial and spiritual crisis.

The truth is that the passage of time alone does not heal the wounds of children of alcoholics. Unless they get help for their deep psychological and spiritual difficulties, they will be at high risk for the development of addiction and/or severe emotional illness *for the rest of their lives.*[3] And chances are, they will pass these problems on to their children and grandchildren, who will become just one more link in a chain of alcoholic damage that stretches from generation to generation.

Fortunately, help is available. There is an effective recovery program for alcoholics—and their families.

14

Five Myths of Addiction

~

The three leading causes of death in the United States are heart disease, cancer, and alcoholism. Among these, alcoholism occupies a unique position: it is completely preventable *and* highly treatable. Almost without exception, any alcoholic who gets appropriate help and is willing to participate in his or her own recovery can lead a sober, productive life.

At the same time, alcoholism is one of the *least* treated of all treatable chronic disorders: less than one in four who need treatment for addictive drinking receive it.[1] Family members, close friends, and employers often share in this paralysis, and no matter how high the price of addiction becomes, they may feel unwilling or unable to effectively intervene in the alcoholic's destructive drinking.

As we explore the recovery process, it is important to appreciate the numerous obstacles that stand between an alcoholic and the help she needs. Some of these barriers have been discussed in previous chapters: the alcoholic's denial, the social stigma attached to addiction, the enabling behavior of family and friends, and the failure of physicians to make a proper diagnosis. Moreover, in one-to-one counseling sessions, the alcoholic is often in the driver's seat, and counselors and therapists without substance abuse training may feed rather than address the alcoholic's delusion. Families in need of help may not be able to afford it, and some have been discouraged by previous treatment failures. For such families, accepting the alcoholic for what he or she is may seem easier than risking another disappointment.

To add to these formidable barriers, there are many widely held myths that discourage people close to an alcoholic from interfering with the course of his or her addictive drinking:

Myth 1: The alcoholic must want help before he can get it. "Every night I begged God to help me," remembered one recovering alcoholic. "I asked God to get me out of trouble, to make me feel better, to not let me die, and to help me get around all the things that stood between me and my next drink. The only thing I never asked God was to help me stop drinking."

It is the rare alcoholic who wants help to quit drinking. Despite periods of desperation and even occasional emotional appeals for assistance, the alcoholic's primary concern is protecting his liquor supply. Many recovering alcoholics testify that even when circumstances compelled them into treatment, they went hoping to find a way to drink without paying the steep price of compulsive drinking. If they had known in advance that recovery required abstinence, they would have stayed home.

Many alcoholics eventually find themselves echoing the desperate prayer of one addicted teacher: "Lord, I need help. I don't want help, but I need help." Meanwhile, family and friends must realize that if they wait for the alcoholic to manifest a sincere desire to quit drinking, her addiction is likely to progress to more serious and untreatable stages. The longer she drinks, the stronger her craving for alcohol becomes, and the less likely it is that she will ever ask for assistance.

Myth 2: The alcoholic must hit rock bottom before she can get help. A distressing number of family members and friends stand by helplessly watching someone they love drink alcoholically because they have heard that alcoholics must hit rock bottom before they can be helped. This "rock bottom" theory was popularized by early groups of Alcoholics Anonymous and was rooted in their experience that only the most desperate and hopeless of circumstances could compel an alcoholic to choose sobriety over alcohol.

It is true that an alcoholic must be allowed to experience the painful consequences of his addiction before he will give up alcohol. But it is also true that alcoholics take their first step toward recovery in part because they fear the loss of something or someone they value. At rock bottom, most alcoholics have nothing to lose—except the comfort of a bottle. Without incentive for becoming sober, they steadily drink themselves toward a bottom from which they cannot return: permanent physical and mental impairment, derangement, institutionalization, and death.

Today we know that the further alcoholics are from the bottom, the greater their chances for achieving sobriety. A drinker who has a family, a job, physical health, friends, and mental clarity has an outstanding chance of recovering from addiction. When his addiction progresses to the point where he loses one or more ingredients of a happy, productive life, his prospects for recovery drop accordingly. If he is sleeping under a bridge, eating food from a can, and talking to himself, there is almost no possibility that he will recover.[2]

Myth 3: The alcoholic will quit drinking on his own. Almost every family of an alcoholic waits expectantly for the day when the alcoholic will spontaneously stop drinking. They have heard stories of other alcoholics who "just up and quit," and they believe that sooner or later the alcoholic in their family will come to his senses. Their hopes may be fueled by the alcoholic's ability to sober up for weeks or months at a time and to act in a responsible way. This behavior may convince family and friends that the alcoholic *could* stop drinking, if only he *would,* and that someday he will choose to sober up.

It is true that some alcoholics spontaneously quit drinking at some time in their lives, often as part of the aging process. However, the vast majority of alcoholics will drink themselves to death unless something or someone interferes with their addiction. With only limited prospects for spontaneous remission, there is no medical or moral justification for watching and waiting while an alcoholic drinks.

Myth 4: The alcoholic has a right to drink, and no one has a right to interfere. "Maya's in rough shape, but if she wants to drink, that's her choice. It's none of our business." I have heard this argument for personal liberty even from fellow physicians. However, the concepts of personal liberty and freedom of choice have little, if any, application to people addicted to chemical substances. While many personal decisions may be involved in the development of an addiction, addiction itself marks the end of free choice. "People choose to be social drinkers," said one recovering alcoholic. "No one chooses to become an alcoholic."

To become an alcoholic is to lose one's ability not to drink. To interfere with the natural course of this addiction is no more an infringement on personal liberty than hospitalizing a person who has threatened suicide or throwing a life preserver to a drowning swimmer. Help may be refused, but the offer is an attempt to restore freedom and dignity, not take it away.

Myth 5: Efforts to help the alcoholic might make her drinking worse. People who live within the orbit of an alcoholic almost always have a paralyzing fear of upsetting the status quo, however unpleasant it may be. Despite the alcoholic's unpredictability, those around her learn to create for themselves islands of stability and order. The peace they find is often as fragile as the relief they feel when the alcoholic drinks herself into a stupor and can be put to bed, but it is still a comfort. The prospect of interfering with the alcoholic's addiction or making changes in the family's routine only raises the frightening specter of a return to chaos.

The alcoholic may play on these fears with remarkable skill. At the first sign of potential interference with his drinking, he may solicit sympathy or imply that he is being "stabbed in the back" by the people he trusts. He may threaten to leave home, to double his drinking, or to physically harm himself or his family. Whatever tactics the alcoholic uses, his message is always the same: there is a price to pay for rocking the boat. (Note: In the presence of threats of suicide and/or violence, family members and friends *must* seek professional assistance, including, where necessary, intervention by law enforcement. This urgent warning to seek help is, of course, easier to give than to follow, and most families will need to seek the support and guidance of professional counselors to find the willingness, practical planning, and courage to take this step.)

The truth is that, while the alcoholic and her enablers fear change, there is seldom any standing still with addiction. Medically speaking, alcoholism is most often a progressive disease. If left to run its course, it gets worse, not better. At any given time, the alcoholic may appear to be holding her own or even recovering, but the overall direction of her life remains the same—downhill. Driven by an overwhelming craving and blinded by denial, she slides into spiritual, psychological, physical, and social devastation. Each aspect of her disease reinforces the others, and she is trapped in a cage that seldom opens from the inside.

Friends and relatives often suffer from the same devastating progression. They may be caught in a paralyzing web of strong and sometimes unconscious emotions, including love, fear, guilt, anger, and a declining sense of self-worth. Their wounded hearts increase their emotional dependence on the alcoholic, and they become less and less able to break free from enabling patterns.

This destructive downward spiral of drinking and enabling will not stop itself. It must be interrupted. The system of relationships that supports the alcoholic's addiction can be transformed. The same family members, friends, and colleagues who shelter the alcoholic can be equipped with the information and tools they need to take charge of their own lives and to help the alcoholic face the serious consequences of addictive drinking.

15

Motivation for Change: First Steps

⁀

The fifty-year-old accountant sitting across from my desk was deeply disturbed. He and his young adult children had come to see me about his wife's drinking problem, but after listening to me outline a program for recovery, he was convinced that I had not understood the seriousness of his wife's condition. "Melissa's case is different," he said emphatically. "She blames everything on me, and if I even mention the word *alcoholic*, she flies into a rage. Whatever you have in mind, I can tell you that it won't work."

Melissa's children echoed their father's hopelessness. Their mother was swinging back and forth between depression and out-of-control behavior. She used Xanax to settle her nerves but was prone to sudden rages during which she physically and verbally abused her husband. Family members tried not to upset Melissa even in small matters, and after fifteen years of living with her addiction, they knew better than to interfere with her drinking. "We appreciate your concern," the eldest son concluded. "But there is no way our mother will ever admit she is an alcoholic, much less accept help."

Like Melissa's husband and children, most people who come through my office have good reason to think a program of recovery won't work for the addicted drinker they love. Their home remedies have failed, they believe they have exhausted their influence with the alcoholic, and they are convinced that he or she has been drinking for too many years to get help. However encouraging I might try to be, the problem remains as real as the disorder of their home life, and the solution seems as remote and ineffective as a fairy tale. Maybe it works for other people, but it will never work for them.

In Melissa's case, her husband and children were desperate enough to try anything. They remained pessimistic about the outcome of their efforts, but they agreed to follow the first steps of a recovery program and prepare themselves to intervene in Melissa's drinking. ("She's too tough," her husband said. "She'll never stand for it.") To their complete astonishment, two months later Melissa was admitted to an outpatient recovery program. During her first week, she threatened to quit the program because she was in the company of "drunks and low-lifes." In the second week, she refused to talk to her family at all, and by the third week, she mentioned plans to get her own apartment. Somewhere in the fourth week, something clicked for Melissa, the "hopeless" alcoholic, and today, after following a comprehensive recovery plan, she has been sober for eighteen years.

The good news about the recovery program for addiction is this: it works. Furthermore, its success doesn't depend on the hopefulness or confidence of family members and friends. Even in the presence of substantial doubt, almost anyone who is willing to follow step-by-step directions can be equipped with effective tools for intervening in the alcoholic's addiction and breaking free from the unhealthy relational dynamics of alcoholism. These efforts are not without difficulties and setbacks, but they take far less energy than living with an addicted drinker year after year. And the potential reward is as great as a new life for the alcoholic, and the emotional and spiritual healing of those who suffer as a result of his or her behavior.

As we begin this how-to portion of our investigation, a word of caution is in order. Although intervening in the life of an addicted drinker can be as brief as a fifteen-minute medical consultation by a doctor trained in the field of substance abuse, it is most often not a one-time event but a *process*. This process requires support, information, and professional guidance. Also, there is no secondhand preparation process, and *reading* is not the same as *doing*. As more than one person has learned from bitter experience, a hasty and ill-informed effort will almost always end in failure and may harm future opportunities to help the alcoholic.

STEP 1: ACCESS SPIRITUAL RESOURCES

Alcoholism and drug addiction are among the most profoundly spiritual of all the problems I deal with as a physician. While reducing addiction to its spiritual dimension is one-sided and ineffective, ignoring or underestimating its spiritual roots is equally dangerous.

It is important for family members and friends to avail themselves of the spiritual resources of their faith tradition, or in the absence of such a tradition, to find other profound sources of comfort, strength, and courage. I ask patients coming from my own religious background to acknowledge their dependence on God and, through prayer, to give themselves and the alcoholic to God's care. Many people are so spiritually drained by years of living with an alcoholic that the only prayer they can manage is "Oh God, if You are there, help me!"

Like an increasing number of medical professionals, I do not see prayer as an afterthought or hopeless last measure to be applied when medicine has failed. Rather, I understand it to be a mysterious but essential healing power in its own right. I would no more be without my ability to pray for, and with, my patients than I would be without my stethoscope. Prayer and science, I have come to believe, are complementary channels of God's grace. It is not that one starts up where the other leaves off, but that both together are agents of divine healing.

STEP 2: GET EDUCATED

Not long ago, I was invited to an association of Protestant ministers to speak on the importance of establishing educational programs about alcoholism within the church. During a question-and-answer time, one man related a disturbing event from the ministry of a fellow pastor:

"Several years earlier, a member of the pastor's congregation was admitted to an alcoholism treatment center at a local hospital. The pastor was skeptical about the concept of 'treatment,' and shortly after the man's admission, the pastor paid him a visit. Signs were posted forbidding visitors during the first ten days, but the pastor was sure they didn't apply to him.

"The pastor met with his parishioner in his room and immediately began lecturing him about his relationship to God and his responsibility to his family. A nurse overheard the pastor's conversation and tried to persuade him to leave. Eventually, she succeeded.

"As the pastor was taking the elevator to his car, his alcoholic parishioner complained that he was thirsty and sent his nurse out for a glass of water. When she returned with the drink, his window was broken and he was lying dead by the door of the pastor's car—seven stories below his room. I wish my pastor friend had known then what I've learned today about addiction."

It is impossible to overemphasize the importance of education for people attempting to help an alcoholic. An enormous amount of damage can be done by well-intentioned but misinformed individuals, and the tragedy is that most of these mistakes could be prevented by a minimal amount of directed study. With a modest educational effort, the minister mentioned above would have known an impor-tant—and in this case, lifesaving—truth: however they present themselves, most alcoholics privately suffer from remorse and despair. Well-meaning helpers can do serious harm to addicted drinkers when they exacerbate the alcoholic's sense of guilt without offering a specific, effective plan of recovery.

For family members in particular, education plays a critical role in the recovery process. When spouses, children, and parents recognize themselves and the alcoholic in the stories of others, their reaction is almost always enormous relief. They realize that they are not alone in their strange dilemma: the behavior that has puzzled and even terrified them for years is part of a universal and diagnosable pattern of addiction. When they learn that this pattern is not unchangeable, their relief turns to cautious hope.

As information leads to understanding, family members and friends acquire some of the emotional detachment necessary to overcome their fear and helplessness. They begin to think more clearly and strategically about the next steps in the recovery program. They also gain essential tools for intervening in the life of an addicted drinker. "Frothy emotional appeal seldom suffices," said the physician whose pioneering efforts inspired the founders of Alcoholics Anonymous. "The message which can interest and hold [alcoholics] must have depth and weight."[1] In my own experience, the effectiveness of family members in the recovery process is directly related to the seriousness with which they have approached their need for education.

A number of outstanding resources for learning the essential facts about alcoholism are listed in Appendix C in the back of this book. Of special importance is the Web site of the National Institute on Alcohol Abuse and Alcoholism: www.niaaa.nih.gov.

STEP 3: FIND A SUPPORT GROUP

Belinda, whose story is told in Chapter 9, clearly remembered her first visit to a family support group. "By then my husband had been drinking alcoholically for thirteen years," she recalled. "But I went to the group to find out how I could keep him from becoming *one of them*. I checked to make sure I didn't recognize any cars in the parking lot and snuck in the back door. If I had been going to a house of prostitution, I couldn't have felt worse.

"The minute I walked into the room, I knew I was in the wrong place. Everyone was laughing and joking, and they looked so relaxed that I was sure none of them had ever lived with a drinker."

Belinda was unimpressed by her first meeting and found several members extremely irritating. Nonetheless, she continued to attend, and every week she heard some story that gave her a new sense of courage and belonging. She was amazed to find other people who felt exactly the way she did: helpless, angry, and guilty.

"But they didn't act like it was my fault that Ben drank," remembered Belinda. "And they didn't make me feel stupid or incompetent because I couldn't handle it. From week to week, I gained confidence. Then one day I discovered that I no longer hated my husband. I saw him as a sick man who didn't want to be the way he was. I also knew that I had found inside myself the strength and serenity I needed to let him experience the consequences of his addiction."

Virtually every community in the United States now has support groups for the family and friends of alcoholics. Some groups are connected with health-care plans, others with treatment centers, community agencies, or even university research programs. Some of these programs are making promising headway in using the insights of cognitive-behavioral therapy to help families intervene in the life of an addicted drinker. But the oldest and best-known family support groups are the 12-step programs of Al-Anon, Alateen, Alakid, and ACOA (Adult Children of Alcoholics).

AL-ANON: A 12-STEP PROGRAM

Al-Anon and other 12-step support groups provide free, accessible support to the families and friends of alcoholics all over the world. Participants meet weekly to "help themselves and others overcome the frustration and helplessness caused by living or having lived with an alcoholic." The healing power of Al-Anon lies not only in acceptance and mutual discovery but in the spiritual power of "The Twelve Steps." These steps, which likewise play a vital role in the recovery of the alcoholic, are discussed in detail in Chapter 21.

As with any self-help movement, some Al-Anon groups are more effective than others, and new research suggests that cognitive and behavioral skills for family members may be more effective for getting an alcoholic into treatment.[2] However, the long-term track record and sustaining power of Al-Anon cannot be dismissed, and like most professionals in the field of substance abuse, I have found that the confidence and effectiveness of family members are usually linked to their willingness to participate in Al-Anon or other 12-step programs. Al-Anon provides a wealth of moral support, information, and practical help for recovery from what it calls "the family disease of addiction." Some Al-Anon literature is designed to be left around the house for the alcoholic's attention.

Note: While relatives and friends of alcoholics may be put off by the individual quirks of a given Al-Anon group, it is important to continue attending meetings. This perseverance requires courage. After years of living with an addicted drinker, family members may perceive themselves as "over and against" other people, rather than as fellow travelers sharing a common experience of suffering and hope. I recommend to all my patients that they attend at least six meetings before they decide that Al-Anon is not for them. By that time, most of them find that the benefits of these meetings far outweigh any drawbacks.

CONTACT INFORMATION

To find an Al-Anon, Alateen, or Alakid meeting near you, call (888)4Al-Anon or contact www.al-anon.alateen.org. The programs are free: there are no dues or membership fees.

A Word of Warning: An addicted drinker may understandably be quite threatened by any effort that upsets the status quo. He or she may go to great lengths to prevent family members from getting the help they need. Family members should consider keeping their initial efforts confidential until they have the internal resources and external support they need to roll with the alcoholic's disapproval or resistance.

One of the more immediate benefits of group membership is that it may equip families to respond with detachment and calm to what may become increasingly hostile or passive-aggressive opposition from the alcoholic. As family members feel more confident, they may want to inform the alcoholic that they are getting help for themselves and learning more about the disorder that is affecting the entire family. They may also find themselves increasingly able to let the addicted drinker experience more fully the negative consequences of addiction.

16

Letting Go

~

Almost all addicted drinkers suffer from the delusion that they are in control of their drinking. This delusion is sustained in part by minimizing the problems caused by addiction.

The opportunity to experience the painful results of addictive drinking is a critical step in the recovery process for the alcoholic (as well as in the recovery of family and friends). As long as an addicted drinker can drink *and* lead a reasonably normal life, she will drink. If suddenly she finds herself dealing alone with the negative consequences of addiction—from cleaning up after herself when she is sick to making her own explanations at work, or even facing legal problems—then she may begin to comprehend the seriousness of her situation. As her illusion of self-control begins to slip, she may become vulnerable enough to accept help for her addiction.

For most people, particularly family members, it is not an easy matter to break old patterns of enabling the alcoholic. Letting go is seldom a painless task in any difficult situation, and to stand aside while the alcoholic suffers genuine pain goes against years of instinctive responses. Disentanglement requires a great deal of prayer, education, and support, and must be grounded in the firm under-standing that the alcoholic will drink herself to a premature death if she does not get help for her drinking.

There are seven key points to keep in mind in this critical stage of letting go and letting the alcoholic experience more profoundly the negative consequences of his or her addictive drinking:

1. *Avoid empty threats and ultimatums.* Don't promise more than you can deliver. If you are emotionally unable to carry out a par-ticular non-enabling step, find the support you need and give yourself time to strengthen your courage and resolve.

2. *Resist the temptation to nag or berate the addicted drinker.* As much as possible, don't allow yourself to be sucked into debates or discussions about the alcoholic's drinking habits. Avoid arguments and fighting; if you can find a quiet center of strength inside your-self, this will send a much stronger message to the alcoholic than any spoken words. In fact, nagging by family members may exacerbate an alcoholic's drinking rather than prevent it. This is, at least in part, because of our human tendency to react against threats to our auton-omy and to increase self-destructive behavior if we think our freedom is being threatened.[1]

3. *Don't hide bottles, pour them out, or measure their contents.* It is not possible to control the alcoholic's drinking by rationing his or her liquor supply, and attempts to do so will likely undermine your efforts to remain emotionally detached.

4. *As far as personal safety permits, be honest and open about your actions.* Think through how you will respond to the alcoholic if he or she inquires about the changes in your behavior. Trust your inner wisdom and your assessment of your specific situation (including any potential for violence) as you frame an answer. For example, you might say, "I've learned some new information about addictive drinking. I love you so much, and I'm sorry that, for all

these years, I've been preventing you from understanding the terrible impact your drinking has had on our family. If you decide you want help for your drinking, I will help you find out how to get the help you need."

As you feel more personally empowered, let the alcoholic know through your words and actions that, while you are deeply disturbed and even pained by the downward spiral of his or her addicted drinking, you have your own life to live and intend to make the most of it.

5. *Provide the alcoholic with information.* Alcoholics Anonymous and Al-Anon provide literature for family members and friends to give to addicted drinkers. It can be an effective intervention simply to leave a pamphlet or two lying around the house where the alcoholic will be sure to see it.

6. *Recognize that the addicted drinker may find temporary (or permanent) new enablers.* It is the rare circle of family and friends that has complete unanimity about how to address the needs of an addicted drinker. As the alcoholic senses the change within people around him, he may attempt to recruit new enablers among family members and friends—and he may succeed. He may even threaten to leave home, although it is unlikely the alcoholic will permanently leave the family on whom he depends for survival. The high-stakes nature of this complicated family interaction underscores the need for professional assistance during this critical stage of intervention.

7. *Get professional help.* The field of substance abuse, like so many other disciplines, is changing rapidly. New technology for exploring the brain has enabled us to map the reward centers of addiction, new drugs are available to combat craving, and advances in our understanding of human motivation and cognitive-behavioral therapy continue to transform intervention and treatment strategies.

At the same time, multiple studies confirm the wisdom and effectiveness of traditional 12-step programs, and AA, Al-Anon, and Alateen continue to play a lifesaving role in the lives of millions of alcoholics around the world.

Sorting out the benefits and drawbacks of these multiple methods and programs can be difficult even for professionals, and family members and friends will find it helpful to engage a doctor, counselor, or substance abuse professional as soon as possible in the recovery process. Trained professionals can help family members and friends explore intervention and treatment options in light of the family's resources, including insurance coverage. They can also provide empathy, objectivity, and optimism at a time when the family's own emotional resources may be at low ebb.

Note: Professional assistance does not need to be long-term or expensive to be effective. Even one or two sessions can provide considerable support, and community agencies often provide family services on a sliding scale. But in two cases professional assistance is *always* required: (1) where there is a threat of violence (including suicide); and (2) where the alcoholic or family members have a co-existing mental health condition, such as depression, bipolar disorder, post-traumatic stress disorder, or schizophrenia.

As family members, close friends, and colleagues put an end to their enabling actions, the alcoholic will become aware of a new wind blowing in his or her life. Occasionally, this awareness alone will prompt the addict to seek help. At other times, the changed behavior of enablers may result in external forces—such as a citation for drunk driving or intervention by an employee assistance program—that compel an alcoholic into treatment.

What can family members and friends do, however, when the alcoholic persists in drinking? It is then time to consider some of the new (and old) tools for intervening in the life of an addicted drinker.

FINDING THE HELP YOU NEED

Finding a qualified professional is usually as simple as checking the yellow pages for the number of a local alcoholism council or treatment center, or networking at a local AA or Al-Anon meeting. It is also possible to call a family physician. (See Appendix C for contact information for helpful national resources.)

What makes a doctor, counselor, or social worker qualified to help family members and friends intervene in the life of an addicted drinker? Here's a short list of what I consider to be the essentials. Professionals must be:

- *trained in the field of substance abuse*

- *empathetic listeners*

- *able to appreciate the spiritual insights and staying power of 12-step programs*

- *familiar with the powerful new research-based tools that are revolutionizing the field of intervention and treatment for addicts. This includes brief intervention, motivational interviewing, cognitive-behavioral therapy, and group interventions*

17

Getting Help:
New Tools for Intervention

~

Jessie, a young mother of three, sat in my office, tapping her foot with irritation. She had been referred to me by her mother, who felt Jessie's drinking was beginning to hurt her grandchildren. Jessie believed that her mother was overreacting and interfering, but privately she, too, was worried that she had become addicted to alcohol.

Jessie's lab work and a brief exam, including alcoholism screening tests, were positive for alcoholism. Jessie listened silently as I explained the serious medical and psychological consequences of addictive drinking, and when I suggested that she enter a local outpatient program, she reluctantly agreed.

Jessie began a recovery program that incorporated a nutrition and exercise component, and when I saw her three months later, her lab work was normal. In subsequent visits, she continued to show improvement, and she is still sober today.

This brief medical intervention is one of several new research-based methods available to doctors and substance abuse professionals working with addicts. These methods, including *motivational interviewing* and advances in cognitive-behavioral therapy, are increasing the rate at which addicted drinkers enter treatment *and* improving their chances of long-term recovery.

BRIEF INTERVENTION

A brief intervention most often takes place in a doctor's office, but in modified form it can also be used by therapists and counselors with a background in substance abuse. Brief interventions may be as short as fifteen minutes or take place over several office visits. In general, they follow a simple pattern:

- With the help of lab tests and alcoholism screening tools, a doctor or substance abuse professional diagnoses addictive drinking.

- The patient is given simple and clear information about the negative medical consequences of alcoholism.

- A referral is made to a treatment program, with follow-up visits to monitor the patient's progress through recovery.

The downside of a brief intervention is that its success depends on the willingness of an addicted drinker to seek *and* follow medical advice. The upside is that, for heavy or addicted drinkers with low levels of denial and high self-motivation for change, it often works, even to the surprise of doctors and family members. In fact, brief intervention is so successful that it has become our most important public health tool in the global effort to reduce alcoholism.[1]

BRIEF INTERVENTION, AA-STYLE

John was lying in a hospital bed, and he had been drinking so heavily that I could still smell the alcohol he was

---

sweating through his skin. He was in his early thirties, and he had fallen from a deck while drinking with friends. I suspected that John was an alcoholic, but it was 1969, and there were no treatment programs available in our city.

In desperation, I called Alcoholics Anonymous. Would they send a recovering alcoholic to come talk with my patient? To my surprise, they agreed. The twelfth step of Alcoholics Anonymous, they informed me, encouraged alcoholics to help other addicted drinkers as part of their recovery program.[2]

A rather undistinguished older gentleman showed up. On his first visit, John was overtly rude—and still quite drunk. But on a second and third visit, John and his uninvited guest began to talk seriously about his addiction. He went straight from the hospital to his first AA meeting, and decades later, he is still sober.

With all the advances in addiction medicine, one recovering alcoholic talking to another still remains one of our most powerful intervention tools. Like any do-it-yourself approach, it has its hazards, dependent as it is on the personalities of the participants and the connection they make with one another. But the upside of this nonprofessional intervention is substantial: it's completely free and thousands of recovering alcoholics can testify to its effectiveness.

A public health note: Cottage Hospital in Santa Barbara, California, has demonstrated the important role that recovering alcoholics and drug addicts can play in emergency room interventions. When hospital administrators learned that more than 80 percent of their weekend admissions were alcohol- or drug-related, they recruited recovering alcoholics and drug addicts to talk to substance-abusing patients. The result: a marked increase in the rate at which addicted patients voluntarily entered treatment programs.

MOTIVATIONAL INTERVIEWING

What motivates people to change? This question lies at the heart of "motivational interviewing," a research-based approach to patients that is bringing new energy to the field of addiction medicine and counseling. Developed by William R. Miller and his colleagues, motivational interviewing is a fundamentally empathic and spiritual approach to human suffering that enables individuals to find within themselves the motivation to change.[3] This approach, studies confirm, increases the odds that alcoholics will enter treatment *and* improves their chances of achieving lasting recovery.

Some basic insights of motivational interviewing include the following:

- Change comes in stages, and gradually.
- By recognizing and responding appropriately to each stage of change, we can increase an alcoholic's motivation to change.
- Aggressive or hostile confrontation methods may *reduce* an alcoholic's willingness to enter treatment.
- Empathy, acceptance, and the confidence that an alcoholic can change are in themselves healing agents. Professionals are successful to the degree that they embody these qualities.

There are many opportunities to use the insights of motivational interviewing in the recovery process, and family members benefit from working with doctors and substance abuse professionals trained in its methods. Helpful resources include the groundbreaking book *Motivational Interviewing: Preparing People for Change* (New York: Guilford Press, 2002) and the Web site www.motivationalinterview.org.

MOTIVATIONAL INTERVIEWING: PRINCIPLES FOR PROFESSIONALS[4]

- *Express empathy through reflective listening.*

- *Enhance the discrepancy between the client's values and [his or her] behavior.*

- *Avoid arguments and direct confrontation.*

- *Roll with resistance rather than oppose it directly.*

- *Support the individual's inner capacity for change.*

COGNITIVE-BEHAVIORAL THERAPY

Cognitive-behavioral therapy, which combines information and skills training, is also helping to shape intervention and treatment programs. A number of studies have shown that when families receive training in life skills that emphasize positive expectations and reinforcement, they can significantly increase the chances that the alcoholic in their lives will enter treatment and begin a recovery program. These techniques have proven particularly successful for parents attempting to get adult children into treatment.[5]

Brief intervention, motivational interviewing, and cognitive-behavioral therapy are all promising approaches for families and professionals working together to intervene in the life of an alcoholic. But what if none of these resources are available to a family or the alcoholic adamantly refuses to get help? In such cases, in my experience, there is still an important role for a well-planned group intervention.

18

Group Intervention:
Love and Honesty

⌣

It was late Sunday morning when Paul arrived at his friend's house for a cup of coffee. He felt sick to his stomach, his head hurt, and he wished he hadn't had so much to drink the night before.

To Paul's surprise, his wife and three children, along with his mother, were sitting in his friend's living room. Paul made a nervous joke, and his friend said, "Paul, we are here because we love and respect you, and we need to tell you something urgent and important."

Paul's wife spoke next, reading from a letter she had written. Her voice was shaking. "Paul, I have always loved you, and I know I always will. We have three beautiful children together. But last Tuesday when we went out to dinner for our anniversary, you poured a bottle of champagne on yourself and made a lewd remark to a woman who walked by our table."

Paul stared at his wife incredulously but was too stunned to respond. His son read next. "Dad, I love you so much, and I've looked up to you for most of my life. But when I brought my fiancée home to meet the family, you were drunk and told an obscene joke.

I know this isn't the real you, Dad, and I hope you will get help for your drinking."

Paul's mother recalled the day he arrived drunk to his parents' fiftieth wedding anniversary and a time he had shoved his father. Paul's friend then read a letter from his medical doctor. "Paul, your high blood pressure makes you a likely candidate for a stroke. Your liver function is seriously impaired, and if you continue to drink, your chances of living another five years are not good. It's a shame, because you are one of the most gifted people I know."

Paul threw up his hands and looked helplessly at the group. "OK, OK," he said with controlled irritation. "I don't know that you went about it right, but I promise that I've had my last drink. You won't see me drunk again."

His friend reminded him of all the previous times that he had promised to quit drinking. There was a long and uncomfortable moment of silence. Then Paul's youngest child, shy and just five years old, spontaneously walked over to her father. She put her hand in his. "Daddy, it's now or never." Paul burst into tears, and within two hours he was in a treatment center. Twenty-five years later, he is still sober.

A SIMPLE PATTERN

Paul's sudden reversal, as startling as it may seem, was no accident. Rather, it was the expected result of a well-planned and rehearsed group intervention that followed specific rules and guidelines. This method was pioneered by the late Dr. Vernon Johnson, who founded the Johnson Institute in Minnesota, and in various modifications it has successfully interrupted the downward spiral of addiction for thousands of alcoholics and their families.

The structure of a group intervention follows a simple pattern. Family members join with other significant people in the alcoholic's life to give feedback about the negative consequences of his drinking. This feedback is loving and nonjudgmental, but firm. As the evidence accumulates, the alcoholic's defense mechanisms give way, and he may be open, at least temporarily, to an offer of outside help.

A WORD OF CAUTION

Carrying out a successful intervention requires careful planning and professional guidance. I once attempted a hastily planned effort at the request of an impatient family, and the result was disastrous. The alcoholic was a close friend of mine, and even before the intervention was under way, he became uncontrollably angry. His threats were so substantial that I required police protection for several days, and he continued to drink until his premature death twenty years later from alcohol-related causes.

It is often the family that suffers most from poor planning. They are operating out of deep distress, and the powerful emotions that spill out during a group intervention can seriously damage or even break apart a family that is not sufficiently prepared.

GUIDELINES FOR GROUP INTERVENTIONS

It takes only one interested person to introduce a family to the group intervention method. Participants must pay careful attention to the following guidelines:

1. *Find professional help.* Although I know of successful group interventions conducted with little outside help, families benefit greatly from working with an experienced substance abuse professional. Family members and friends are often so emotionally enmeshed with the alcoholic that it is difficult for them to provide the calm, respectful, and loving leadership that is required. Professional third parties can evaluate the risk factors (see below), remain detached if the situation becomes highly volatile, and help the

family understand treatment options in light of insurance issues and financial resources.

To find a qualified doctor or counselor who understands the dynamics of both addiction and group intervention, a number of excellent resources are available. These include local substance abuse councils, Alcoholics Anonymous, the American Society of Addiction Medicine, the Salvation Army, and the Hazelden Foundation, a well-established pioneer in the field of addiction and intervention. There are also a growing number of professional "interventionists" who charge from $500 to $2,500 or more.

Note: The Hazelden Foundation has published a detailed and helpful book about group interventions, *Love First*, by Jeff and Debra Jay (Center City, MN: Hazelden, 2000).

PROFESSIONAL RESOURCES: CONTACT INFORMATION

Alcoholics Anonymous
www.alcoholics-anonymous.org

American Society of Addiction Medicine
www.asam.org
(301) 656-3920

Hazelden Foundation
www.hazelden.org
(800) 257-7810

The Salvation Army
www.salvationarmy.org

The Intervention Resource Center
www.interventioninfo.org

---

2. *Choose the intervention team.* Participants in a group intervention are selected on the basis of their relationship with the alcoholic and their willingness to help. Not all friends or family members will approve of a group intervention (some may even try to sabotage it), but with education a surprising number of people are willing to help.

The most strategic participants are usually the alcoholic's significant other (spouse, parent, or child), a close friend, a sympathetic employer, and the alcoholic's doctor, if he or she is knowledgeable about addiction. Although few doctors will attend an intervention, they can be present through a letter read by the group leader. A recovering alcoholic who is a friend of the alcoholic can also be an effective team member.

Other potential participants are children, relatives, and faith leaders. There is no age requirement, and children should not be excluded simply on the basis of age.[1] Even young children are often painfully aware of their family's drinking problem, and like Paul's daughter, they may make a life-changing contribution.

Individuals who should be *excluded* from the intervention team include:

- those whose psychological states are too fragile to withstand the emotional impact of the intervention;
- anyone likely to berate the alcoholic or preach to her in moralistic tones;
- those whose anger or hostility makes it difficult for them to speak to the addicted drinker with love and respect.

At the same time, there are no perfect members of an intervention team, and seemingly ineffective people often play important roles. I once selected a twenty-year-old woman, on the basis of her emotional maturity and stability, to participate in a group intervention with her alcoholic mother. The young woman broke down when her mother walked into the room, cried throughout the entire meeting, and was unable to read her letter. The mother was so moved by the tears of her otherwise stoic daughter that she agreed to begin a recovery program.

In my experience, the optimum number of participants in an intervention is four to six people, including the professional counselor. It is possible, but not ideal, to do an intervention with as few as two people and, occasionally, with as many as eight.

3. *Write a letter.* Each participant writes a brief letter to the alcoholic that includes one or more examples of the alcoholic's inappropriate behavior under the influence of alcohol. These examples need to be as detailed, current, and colorful as possible, with a focus on factual information rather than negative feelings and judgments. For instance, a statement like, "You always embarrass me in public, and I'm sick and tired of it!" is better said, "Last month at the Jacksons' party, you were sick all over their new carpet, and here is the cleaning bill they sent us."

Keep in mind that the purpose of this data is not to humiliate the alcoholic but to help her see the true seriousness of her addictive behavior. Angry, hostile remarks will activate the alcoholic's natural and formidable defense mechanisms, but evidence given with loving concern enables her to consider, at least for a moment, the truth of the information she receives.

A letter from a doctor should be factual and informative. My own approach is to start with the brain and descend down the human body, giving a list of physical damage that is tailored to the alcoholic's own health issues. In the context of a group intervention, it is often easier for the alcoholic to digest the true gravity of her physical condition.

Warning: The professional counselor must listen carefully to the history of the alcoholic's behavior provided by family members. If there is a potential for violence or suicide, or if the alcoholic is using alcohol as self-medication for a mental illness, a group intervention may not only be counterproductive but dangerous. If possible, the alcoholic should be directed to seek help from a reputable psychiatrist or mental health institution.

4. *Choose the time and place.* A group intervention should be carried out at a time of day when the alcoholic is sober, or as sober as possible. If participants discover that the alcoholic is drunk at the scheduled hour, I recommend postponing the intervention. In my experience, Sunday morning after a bad drinking weekend is an unusually effective time. Night meetings, on the other hand, tend to be dangerous and should be avoided if possible.

It is helpful to hold a group intervention away from the alcoholic's residence, preferably at the home of a friend or family member, or even in a medical office. On neutral ground, the alcoholic may be less defensive and more constrained in his behavior.

5. *Hold a practice intervention.* Members of the intervention team need to meet at least once, and preferably twice, to rehearse the intervention. During these meetings the professional counselor plays the role of the alcoholic, and team members practice giving their evidence in a detached, nonjudgmental manner. Participants may experience unexpected and powerful emotions, and they can take this opportunity to express their ambivalence and hesitations.

Under the counselor's supervision, team members practice responding, or not responding, to a variety of positions the alcoholic may take. She may express strong feelings of betrayal, be openly hostile or aggressive, or try to deflect the seriousness of the situation with humor or false compliance: "You're right, I'm a hopeless alcoholic," or, like Paul: "Maybe I do have a drinking problem. I'll quit today!" When team members prepare in advance for a variety of responses, they are less likely to be caught off guard or to give their power away to the addicted drinker.

It is family members who benefit the most from a practice session. They are normally terrified of the coming intervention and certain it will fail, but as the rehearsal progresses, they visibly gain confidence and determination. It may have been years since they talked openly about the behavior of the alcoholic, and they may have concealed from one another many difficult and painful experiences. Now, through honest conversation, their family bonds deepen. And as they pool their evidence, even the most lukewarm participants become convinced that the alcoholic is seriously ill and in need of immediate help.

19

Decision Time

∿

Whatever method of intervention we use to interrupt the cycle of addiction, and however careful our planning, every intervention is a voyage into the unknown. An addicted drinker who seems totally resistant may immediately agree to enter a treatment program, while a seemingly compliant and congenial alcoholic might offer unexpected resistance. Sooner or later, every alcoholic must come to his or her own decision, a highly personal action that others cannot control.

At the same time, by participating in a group intervention, family and friends serve notice that change is unavoidable. They will not continue to support the alcoholic in his continued drinking, and the addict must now choose his next step from a limited number of options. The intervention team explores these options in advance so that they can, in turn, respond appropriately to the alcoholic's decision.

OUTCOME 1: WHAT IF THE ALCOHOLIC AGREES TO ACCEPT HELP?

There is much about a successful intervention that at first glance seems startling and inexplicable. An alcoholic stubbornly committed to drinking, no matter how devastating the consequences, suddenly agrees to get help. This reversal, which happens in three of four well-planned group interventions, is so unexpected that family members and friends may have trouble believing the evidence of their own ears.

The keys to the addicted drinker's sudden change of heart are the spiritual power of a loving, respectful group intervention and the alcoholic's own inner torment. While an alcoholic may go to great lengths to appear confident and independent, he is acutely aware of how untenable his position is—he can't live without alcohol, and he can't live with it. He is terrified of his life as an addict, but he is equally terrified of losing his supply of alcohol. His growing anxiety is aggravated by his awareness that he cannot take care of himself while he is drinking and by the fear that he will lose the people who support him in his addiction. Even as these tensions escalate, he continues to drink a chemical that produces the very anxiety it is meant to relieve.

When members of the intervention team are able temporarily to put aside their own frustrations and speak to the suffering addict out of loving concern, they create enormous energy for change. "Most of us will live and die and never experience a time when the people we care about come together in one room, at one time, to tell us how much they love us and why," reflected interventionists Jeff and Debra Jay, authors of *Love First*. "As you can imagine, this is an overwhelmingly emotional encounter for an alcoholic who feels anything but loveable."[1] When this experience includes a practical offer of help, the addicted drinker often finds the motivation he or she needs, at least temporarily, to enter treatment.

There are three basic treatment options, and the intervention team determines in advance the course of action they will recommend:

- an intensive outpatient program, including detoxification;
- inpatient care at an alcoholism treatment center; or

- Alcoholics Anonymous—ninety meetings in ninety days.

These programs, with their pros and cons, are discussed more fully in Chapter 21. The team makes their choice based on the individual needs and financial resources (including insurance) of the addicted drinker, as well as the availability of treatment programs. Alcoholics who have been addicted for years and whose families are severely wounded by their behavior, most often need a longer course of treatment and do best with options one or two. Alcoholics who have a low level of denial and strong self-motivation may do well simply attending Alcoholics Anonymous, after they have been through detoxification in a hospital or treatment center.

Note: Under no circumstances should an alcoholic withdraw from alcohol without professional supervision and medication. In the presence of a coexisting mental illness, the alcoholic *must* be treated in a setting where their medications can be carefully monitored and coordinated by mental health professionals.

Plans for admission to an inpatient or outpatient program should be made in advance, preferably for the same day as the intervention, but always as soon as possible. The less time the addicted drinker has to reconsider, the better. During planning, team members should anticipate the alcoholic's objections to immediate treatment and role-play their responses. They also need to arrange coverage for the alcoholic's work responsibilities and other commitments.

OUTCOME 2: WHAT IF THE ALCOHOLIC REFUSES HELP BUT PROMISES TO QUIT DRINKING?

Sometimes interventions end with the addicted drinker refusing to get outside help but promising that he will quit drinking on his own. If, after reasonable efforts, the alcoholic continues to resist treatment options, the intervention team should consider the following steps:

1. *Avoid attacking the alcoholic; express appreciation for any concessions he makes.* Alcoholic denial is so strong that even an indirect admission of a drinking problem can be a giant first step.

2. *Ask the alcoholic to enter into a verbal agreement with the intervention team.* In this agreement, the alcoholic tries to quit drinking on her own and agrees that if she begins drinking again, she will get outside help without delay.

Although the alcoholic may sincerely believe that "this time it will be different," it is unlikely that she will be able to stop drinking on her own. Normally it is only a matter of time before she has a major slip. When not drinking by sheer willpower, an alcoholic suffers from what is commonly called the *dry-drunk syndrome.* Her constant craving for alcohol forces her to expend so much energy *not* drinking that she can think of little else. Because alcohol is still the center of her life, her addictive behavior remains the same, or she may become even more irritable and agitated. It is difficult, if not impossible, to stay in this state indefinitely. In almost every case, the pressure of craving combines with work and family stresses to compel the alcoholic to take "just one more drink."

3. *Before closing the intervention, find a way to let the alcoholic know he is loved and respected* and that team members empathize with the struggle addiction creates. Keep the doors of communication open, and avoid implying that the alcoholic has failed or that he is now rejected by his family or friends.

OUTCOME 3: WHAT IF THE INTERVENTION DOESN'T SUCCEED?

Occasionally an alcoholic storms out of an intervention before it is completed or refuses to comply in any way with the requests of the intervention team. In such cases, the group has several options:

1. If possible, try the intervention again. Occasionally, when a first intervention fails, a second one succeeds.

2. Be patient. Don't underestimate the power of time and the alcoholic's own anxiety. While the addicted drinker may appear hardened and unreachable during the group intervention, in all likelihood he is hearing and digesting an unsettling amount of information. One of my patients, a young man of eighteen, sat through a New Year's Eve intervention in sullen silence and went out drinking the minute we finished talking. "It was the worst night of my life," he remembered. "For the first time since I became an alcoholic, I knew in my heart that I was doing something wrong. I drank more than ever, trying to kill the pain, but it wouldn't go away. After two days of drinking, I went into treatment."

3. Prior to the intervention, think through responses to a refusal to get help. Does the husband or wife plan to stay with the alcoholic? Do the children intend to continue living at home? Does the employer plan to terminate the alcoholic's job? The options available to families are discussed more fully in Chapter 26. Employers should be aware that their mere presence at a group intervention considerably raises the possibility of a positive outcome. The threat of losing a job is a powerful incentive, and alcoholics are likely to accept help if their jobs are at stake.

4. Remember that even if the alcoholic never quits drinking, an intervention is almost always a time of healing and reconciliation for family members. One of my saddest and most difficult group interventions was with four teenagers whose parents were both alcoholics. Their father came close to accepting help but at the last minute was intimidated by threats from his wife. A wealthy uncle who financially supported the family participated in the intervention but refused the children's request to stop sending their father money. The intervention ended when we were thrown out of the house. The children were in tears, and their mother followed us down the road, threatening retaliation. Both parents continued to drink, and within two years, both of them had died from alcohol-related health problems.

The value of that distressing and seemingly unsuccessful intervention was immeasurable. During the practice session, two of the children discovered that they themselves were addicts—one to cocaine, one to alcohol. Both went into treatment, and today all four children are chemical free and deeply connected to one another. The children's grandparents, who had been unaware of their tragic home life, stepped in to give them the love and support they needed. Shortly after the group intervention, the eldest son came to my office. He spoke of the mix of sadness and relief that he felt now that he had done everything possible to help his parents. "I know they probably will never stop drinking," he said. "I'm not happy about the decisions they have made, but I feel like a heavy load has dropped off my back. My parents' drinking no longer has the power to destroy me. I've done my part, and now I'm free to get on with my own life."

OUTCOME 4: WHAT IF A GROUP INTERVENTION IS NOT POSSIBLE?

Occasionally it is impossible to carry out a group intervention. In this case, it is important to be flexible and creative. One of my most gratifying interventions involved the simple gesture of giving an alcoholic friend a copy of *Dying for a Drink*. She read it, called me for the name of a treatment center, packed her bags, went into treatment, and remained sober the rest of her life.

On another occasion, just prior to a group intervention, a woman telephoned to say that her husband was threatening me with physical harm if I showed up at their house. The intervention was canceled, but the husband called the following day and angrily demanded to know why his wife was consulting me. I explained that his addiction was a cause for concern and that there was help available if he was interested. The man agreed to enter a treatment program, and to my surprise, he kept his promise.

These examples are not models to follow, but they illustrate that interventions do not have to be ideal to be successful. Sometimes an unusual moment here or there will break through the alcoholic's denial and bring him to the next important step in his recovery process, the willingness to accept outside help.

20

Some Words of Caution

~

When painful circumstances or an organized intervention compel an addicted drinker to seek treatment, she and her family and friends face some important questions: Where does an alcoholic go to learn how to quit drinking? What kind of help does she need?

Before we examine in detail the treatment options available to alcoholics, there are several points to keep in mind:

1. *No addicted drinker should be left alone during physical withdrawal.* Alcohol is a depressant, and its habitual use leads to physical dependence. This dependence results from the chronic depression of normal activity in the central nervous system and the adjustments it makes to adapt to the constant presence of alcohol. When alcohol is suddenly withdrawn, the central nervous system rebounds into hyperactivity, and the alcoholic experiences withdrawal symptoms ranging in severity from irritability and nervousness to seizures and life-threatening delirium tremens (DT's).[1] The most common withdrawal symptoms are increased blood pressure, profuse sweating, rapid heartbeat, sleeplessness, and tremulousness, or "the shakes."

Withdrawal symptoms normally last two to three days, but they can persist for two or three weeks. The severity of these symptoms is usually related to how long and how much the alcoholic has been drinking, but occasionally even short-term drinkers have serious or life-threatening complications. *The death rate for unassisted alcohol withdrawal is higher than the rate for heroin withdrawal,* and every alcoholic must be given the appropriate medications and monitored closely to prevent the onset of DT's. With medical assistance, withdrawal is most often a straightforward process.

Before beginning a group intervention, it is important for the intervention team to identify a detoxification center, either in a treatment facility or at a hospital. During withdrawal, the alcoholic needs constant reassurance and loving support to help reduce her anxiety and fear. A special effort should be made to explain the nature of her physical symptoms and the purpose of any necessary medical interventions. Members of Alcoholics Anonymous are often available to sit with an alcoholic during withdrawal, and help can be obtained by calling a local chapter of AA.

2. *An alcoholic's recovery is usually connected to his ability to perceive his addiction as a disease.* The most common objection to the disease model of addiction is that alcoholics may use it as a means of avoiding responsibility for their drinking. In my experience, this criticism is almost entirely hypothetical. I have never known an alcoholic who rationalized his drinking by blaming it on the *disease* of alcoholism. In fact, the opposite is true. Alcoholics are usually the last people to admit that they have a disease, and it is only when they finally accept this concept that they are able to take constructive steps toward recovery.

"You can't imagine the relief I felt when I learned I had a disease that afflicted millions of people," said one recovering alcoholic. "It was like a burden of despair and loneliness fell from my back. I wasn't paralyzed by guilt anymore, and for the first time in years I thought about the future. I could think through the steps I needed to take to recover."

3. *There is no known cure for alcohol addiction.* Alcoholism, like diabetes, most often is a progressive, chronic disorder that can be controlled or arrested, but not cured. In almost every case, the brain changes created by addiction are lifelong. While it is thought that a small percentage of alcoholics can return to social drinking after developing an addiction, the vast majority of alcoholics, *for the remainder of their lives*, will only be able to control their craving for alcohol by *not drinking*. At one time or another, most alcoholics will be tempted to think of themselves as the rare exception; the overwhelming majority will be wrong.

In my own faith community, the notion of the incurability of alcoholism is occasionally controversial. "Sometimes a Christian friend tries to convince me that I'm not *recovering*; I'm *healed*," an addicted friend told me. "I believe in healing, and sometimes I'm tempted to believe him. Why not take a little glass of wine? After all, other Christians drink socially; why can't I? Then I remember. I *am* an alcoholic. God has healed me from my burning compulsion for alcohol, but all my life I'm going to be just one drink away from a drunk."

A WORD ABOUT "INSTANT HEALING"

There is no question that some people are miraculously and instantly healed from a seemingly incurable, fatal illness. These are the kind of experiences we wish happened frequently, but they are rare, and the possibility of such a healing does not relieve patients of the responsibility of seeking medical help and participating in their own health care. The diabetic waiting for healing is responsible for controlling her diet and using insulin when needed. Likewise, the alcoholic, her family members, and her friends have a responsibility to make use of the time-tested tools for recovery from addiction. People who encourage an alcoholic to search for an instant healing when a proven program of recovery is available are participating in a dangerous and potentially fatal form of enabling. They feed the alcoholic's delusion of being an exception to the rule and prevent her from getting the help that can save her life.

My professional experience has taught me that alcoholics who believe they have been healed may do well for a few weeks or months, but sooner or later the wheels start coming off, and the craving to drink returns. Alcoholism is a holistic disorder, and both the alcoholic and his family must contend with the serious emotional, spiritual, and relational consequences of addiction. These consequences don't disappear overnight, and without adequate tools for recovery, alcoholics are caught off guard by persisting problems. At this stage, even someone who has been miraculously delivered from a physical craving for alcohol is likely to turn to a bottle to find the consolation and courage he needs.

With these cautionary reflections in mind, it is time to turn our attention to the question of treatment. Where do alcoholics go to get help for their addiction?

21

Paths to Sobriety

~

Rebecca began drinking in response to a stressful marriage. She was in her third week at a treatment program when a counselor asked her what she would do if her husband's behavior didn't improve. "I said I didn't know," Rebecca recalled. "Then she asked me again, and a light went on in my head. I knew what I was going to do: I was going to take a drink.

"As soon as I said this out loud, I realized that I wasn't locked in anymore. I had a choice. Even if my husband never changed, I had tools for sobriety, a support group, and a deepening relationship with God. It was a long time before our home life improved, and I was always grateful for that moment when I learned that I was no longer dependent on alcohol."

Rebecca's journey of self-discovery demonstrates the ongoing jeopardy of recovering alcoholics and the importance of finding effective methods for staying sober. The moment of insight that an addicted drinker has during an intervention, however deeply felt, is almost always fleeting. When the alcoholic's physical craving for alcohol returns and relationship problems persist, she must have at hand tools that are as powerful as her addiction. It is these tools that a good treatment program can provide.

Currently there are three well-tested treatment options to help alcoholics find the holistic healing they need. Some may be tempted to follow less-tested methods or even paths of their own devising, and perhaps here and there such efforts will be successful. Recovery rates, however, are on the side of well-established treatment programs with research-based protocols, including attendance at Alcoholics Anonymous. As one recovering alcoholic said, "If you come to an uncharted minefield and see footprints, you had better follow them—very closely."[1]

OPTION 1: INTENSIVE OUTPATIENT CARE

Outpatient programs are connected with treatment centers or hospitals and often include detoxification facilities. They usually offer day and night programs to accommodate work schedules, and recovering alcoholics remain in the program from six weeks to several months.

Like inpatient programs, the best outpatient programs create an atmosphere of loving acceptance, honest self-assessment, and high expectations. As the alcoholic comes to terms with the gravity of her addiction, she learns new methods of communication, how to ask for help, and tools for handling disappointment and anxiety without resorting to drinking. She may be asked to work through the first steps of the Twelve Steps of Alcoholics Anonymous.

Most outpatient and inpatient programs also offer a family program to help family members in their own recovery process. Studies confirm that effective family programs not only help families stay together but also increase the chances that the alcoholic will achieve sobriety.

Many insurance policies cover outpatient treatment, and there are some excellent nonprofit or government-funded programs.

To find out about accredited programs in your area, contact
www.recoverynetwork.com. Members of Alcoholics Anonymous may
also be a good resource for learning the inside story on various treatment programs.

Note: An eight-year study by the National Institute on Alcohol
Abuse and Alcoholism (NIAAA) has found that 12-step programs,
cognitive-behavioral therapy, and motivational-enhancement therapy
were equally effective in treating alcoholism. In my view, the best
treatment programs combine insights from many different fields and
approaches, and include a focus on nutrition and exercise.

TREATMENT PROGRAMS: INGREDIENTS FOR SUCCESS

*The elements of a successful recovery program are the same for both
outpatient and inpatient centers. These include:*

- *guided small groups and individual counseling;*

- *cognitive-behavioral therapy, including life skills
  training, nutrition counseling, exercise, and relapse
  prevention;*

- *supervision of appropriate medications;*[2]

- *wraparound services where needed (social services,
  psychiatric care for coexisting mental illness, job
  training, etc.);*

- *an introduction to Alcoholics Anonymous and other
  12-step programs;*

- *a family program for family members and friends;*

- *an extensive aftercare program.*

OPTION 2: INPATIENT TREATMENT

The advantages of outpatient treatment are that the recovering addict can live at home and keep working, and he learns his recovery skills in the context of his daily life. The disadvantage is the absence of a controlled environment during the first critical weeks of recovery. As an outpatient, the addicted drinker is bombarded by all kinds of stimuli that trigger his craving, including his old drinking friends. Many an alcoholic has returned to addictive drinking in the first few weeks of recovery just because he mistakenly believed he could go to a bar and order a soft drink.

Inpatient treatment, on the other hand, provides the addict with a structured, simplified environment in which he has few decisions to make and no access to alcohol or drugs. The most common triggers for relapse are removed, and the addict is able to focus all his energies on recovery.

The serious downside of inpatient treatment is the cost, and few insurance programs cover inpatient care except in the face of repeated relapse—and sometimes not even then. There are, however, excellent nonprofit inpatient programs that operate on a sliding scale, and some offer scholarships or creative financing. An addiction counselor can help families and friends identify potential inpatient centers.

Note: Admission arrangements to both inpatient and outpatient programs should be made in advance of an intervention, and when possible the addicted drinker should go straight to treatment. The less time the alcoholic has to rethink, the better.

For alcoholics and their families with limited financial means and no insurance, there is a third option: attending ninety meetings of Alcoholics Anonymous in ninety days. Alcoholics Anonymous can provide some (but not all) of the resources of inpatient or outpatient care, and it has the advantage of being completely free.

THERAPEUTIC COMMUNITIES

Substance abuse treatment is costly, and the trend in managed care is toward the short term. There is substantial data, however, that suggests people need more treatment, rather than less. In fact, some of the best recovery rates come from "therapeutic communities" or halfway houses, where recovering addicts share living space with counselors who help them address multiple levels of need over an extended period of time.

OPTION 3: ALCOHOLICS ANONYMOUS

In 1935, two hard-drinking alcoholics, whom doctors had long dismissed as hopeless drunks, set out on a bold venture to help each other stop drinking. Four years later, they were surrounded by more than a hundred recovering alcoholics, and they could write:

> Rarely have we seen a person fail who has thoroughly followed our path. Those who do not recover are people who cannot or will not completely give themselves to this simple program, usually men and women who are constitutionally incapable of being honest with themselves . . . There are those, too, who suffer from grave emotional and mental disorders, but many of them do recover if they have the capacity to be honest.[3]

The work of these two men, and the organization they founded, is the primary reason why alcoholism today is no longer considered a hopeless condition. The success of AA, which functions without rules, officers, or advertisement, is so substantial that almost every treatment center in the world sends its patients to AA as part of their recovery process.

At the heart of AA's effectiveness are twelve simple steps. These steps, restatements of profound Judeo-Christian-Islamic principles, are simple enough for the foggiest alcoholic to understand and so complex that their spiritual riches cannot be exhausted in a single lifetime. The Twelve Steps have been applied effectively to many kinds of addictive behavior, including overeating, gambling, sex addiction, and most recently, compulsive Internet use.

THE TWELVE STEPS[1]

1. We admitted we were powerless over alcohol—that our lives had become unmanageable.

2. Came to believe that a Power greater than ourselves could restore us to sanity.

3. Made a decision to turn our will and our lives over to the care of God as we understood God.

4. Made a searching and fearless moral inventory of ourselves.

5. Admitted to God, to ourselves, and to another human being the exact nature of our wrongs.

6. Were entirely ready to have God remove all these defects of character.

7. Humbly asked God to remove our shortcomings.

8. Made a list of all persons we had harmed, and became willing to make amends to them all.

---

9. Made direct amends to such people wherever possible, except when to do so would injure them or others.

10. Continued to take personal inventory and when we were wrong promptly admitted it.

11. Sought through prayer and meditation to improve our conscious contact with God as we understood God, praying only for knowledge of God's will for us and the power to carry that out.

12. Having had a spiritual awakening as the result of these steps, we tried to carry this message to alcoholics, and to practice these principles in all our affairs.

Members of AA help one another "grow along spiritual lines" through weekly meetings, one-on-one sponsorship, and answering calls for help, twenty-four hours a day, from recovering alcoholics suffering from craving or other problems. The atmosphere of an AA meeting, at its best, is a mixture of loving acceptance, laughter, and honest communication. For AA members, the knowledge that they share a dangerous addiction creates a beloved community seldom found in contemporary Western society.

The kindness and understanding a visiting alcoholic finds at AA often draws her back to meetings over and over again, even while she is mentally dissociating herself from "those crazy drunks." The acceptance she receives bolsters her declining self-esteem, and over a period of time, she finds more and more pieces to the puzzle of her addiction. Veteran members share their own struggles with the power of physical craving, self-deception, self-centeredness, spiritual destitution, and other consequences of addiction. When the alcoholic begins to see herself in others, the walls of her denial may crumble, and she may admit that she, too, is powerless over alcohol.

When an alcoholic admits that her life is unmanageable and turns her life over to a Higher Power, she begins the hard process of admitting her faults, making restitution to people she has wronged, strengthening her relationship with God, and helping other alcoholics. There are no rules in AA to tell a recovering alcoholic how to carry out the Twelve Steps, but a large body of collected wisdom and oral history help her make practical applications to her own life. Her efforts to help other nonrecovering alcoholics remind her of the nightmare from which she has narrowly escaped, and with the guidance of older members of AA, she learns the art of staying sober "one day at a time."

STRENGTHS AND WEAKNESSES

The great strengths of Alcoholics Anonymous are that it works and it's free. The drawbacks are that AA lacks the individual and multidisciplinary approach of treatment programs, and there is no systematic education about addiction. The alcoholic's education depends on the experience and wisdom of his fellow alcoholics, and while their knowledge is often substantial, they may have considerable blind spots and biases.

Despite these drawbacks, AA is often a reliable alternative to a treatment center, and ongoing participation in its program is an important part of recovery for most alcoholics. There are AA meetings in all major cities and most small towns, and information on available groups can be obtained at www.alcoholics-anonymous.org, or by calling local phone listings for Alcoholics Anonymous. You may also write to Alcoholics Anonymous World Services, Inc., Box 459, Grand Central Station, New York, NY 10163.

Note: The success of AA is based on principles, not personalities. If an alcoholic is bothered by certain individuals in his group, he can change groups or learn to put up with people he doesn't like for the sake of his sobriety. Every alcoholic should be encouraged to attend at least six meetings of AA before deciding on its usefulness. In most cases, an alcoholic's refusal to attend AA is rooted in pride and embarrassment, or the unacknowledged need to feel exceptional. I have found that most patients who stick with AA for a few months begin to see it as an essential tool in their recovery program.

HIGHER POWER

Some recovering alcoholics are turned off by the spiritual language of the Twelve Steps, either because it is too specific or too vague. Alternative 12-step programs have been started for people who do not believe in the existence of a "Higher Power" and who think that this belief perpetuates a paralyzing sense of victimhood and helplessness. Human beings, these groups believe, are rational beings who have all they need inside their own minds and with the help of friends to recover from addiction. The founding philosopher of this movement is psychologist Albert Ellis, and there are now a number of "rational recovery" groups.

At the same time, there are some faith groups who feel the phrase "Higher Power" is offensive because it does not use the language of their faith commitment. From my view as a physician and a person of faith, I believe this view is shortsighted and even dangerous, because it prevents people from getting lifesaving help. Alcoholics Anonymous has helped hundreds of thousands of alcoholics from all religious persuasions, and I have never known any alcoholic whose faith was damaged by the program. In fact, the opposite is true: most alcoholics deepen their faith commitments while working through the Twelve Steps. "Alcoholics Anonymous won't get you to heaven, and it can't keep you out of hell," one recovering alcoholic told me, "but it can keep you sober long enough to make up your own mind."

The historical reality is that alcoholics repeatedly turned for help to the helping professions, to doctors and faith leaders, and received no help at all. So, out of desperation, they turned to one another, and from their fellowship and mutual support came Alcoholics Anonymous. From this group of people whom everyone else dismissed as completely hopeless, AA has produced a vast network of recovering alcoholics. The testimony of these transformed lives cannot be rejected out of hand, and in my own view, it is a cause for celebrating the transforming work of God in the world.

When I was a kid, I was jealous of my friends and their families. Our house was just a place to eat and sleep; we didn't talk to each other. At meals, everyone was quiet—unless there was an all-out war. It got so I was only happy when I was drunk, and I became an alcoholic before I was thirteen.

When my parents found out, they made me go to a treatment center, and they went to Al-Anon. That's how they figured out that they were alcoholics too. So they started going to AA meetings. Today, things are different in our family. We sit down for meals together. We joke around and talk things over. It's the little things we do as a family—like going out and stuff. Mostly now I take it for granted, but sometimes when I think about it, I start to cry.

—DANIEL, age 16

22

When the Honeymoon Ends

~

Travis was a bright, talented adolescent who began compulsive drinking at the age of sixteen. For the next twenty-two years, alcohol was the center of his life. He drifted in and out of marriage and for a brief time even lived in a homeless shelter.

In his late thirties, Travis had a spiritual conversion, married, and became a father. He went back to school to get a business degree and quickly developed a successful marketing company. He was elected to a leadership position within his church and started a mission for homeless people.

"I looked good and sounded good, and everyone assumed I knew what I was doing," recalled Travis. "In fact, after twenty-two years of addiction, I had the emotional maturity of a teenager, with no idea how to handle adult responsibilities.

"I felt so trapped that I began fantasizing about living on the street again, where my only worry was finding the next drink," he added. Travis went to a doctor, complaining of insomnia, and within six months he had a new problem: addiction to Xanax. His marriage and company quickly began to unravel. "Now when I imagined myself on the street, it wasn't a pleasant fantasy but a frightening possibility," Travis said. "I was terrified but too proud and ashamed to ask for help."

Travis's wife eventually convinced him to see a therapist, and after three hospitalizations and intensive substance-abuse treatment, he was finally drug free. "Addiction to pills was a logical progression of my alcoholism," reflected Travis. "I stopped drinking, but I never grew up. I responded to everything based on my feelings, and it never occurred to me that I could have strong emotions and not act on them. At the age of forty-six I began learning the life lessons that most people learn as young adults."

Travis's story follows a common pattern found in the lives of recovering alcoholics. The first few weeks or months of sobriety bring rapid progress: the recovery of physical health and mental clarity, the absence of blackouts and lost weekends, and a deep joy that resembles the euphoria of early drinking days. The recovering alcoholic is high on being sober, and although in the back of his mind he has a nagging fear of relapse, he may think and act with the reckless abandon of a new convert.

Sooner or later, however, for every recovering alcoholic, the honeymoon comes to an end. For some it dies abruptly when, from seemingly out of nowhere, a physical craving for alcohol returns with overwhelming intensity. For others, like Travis, there is the gradual but unsettling return of old problems, coupled with new adult responsibilities. Everywhere the recovering alcoholic looks there are bridges to build and fences to mend. He may have a deep physical lethargy and mental fog that lasts for a year or more, his marriage relationship may be rocky, and his children may begin to express previously hidden resentments and hostility.

In many ways the recovering alcoholic is an amnesia victim, a chemical Rip Van Winkle who returns to life five, ten, or even forty years later to discover that a large segment of his adult life has disappeared. There may be deaths he never mourned, weddings and birthday parties he did not attend, perhaps even criminal behavior that has gone unaddressed. Lost years with family members, particularly children, cannot be recovered, and the newly sober alcoholic is often overwhelmed with grief when he realizes how much of his young adulthood is gone.

In the face of grief, family problems, and adult responsibilities, the recovering alcoholic is handicapped by inadequate emotional development. As a general rule, maturation ends when addiction begins, and the child, teenager, or adult who learns to solve his problems by swallowing a chemical almost always falls far behind his peers in wisdom and the ability to handle difficulties. Travis became an alcoholic at sixteen. Twenty-two years later, when he finally sobered up, he still thought and acted like a teenager. Unlike alcoholics who become addicted later in life, he had few *learned adult behaviors* to which he could return. He did not know how to handle anxiety and pressure without drinking, he was accustomed to quick answers and shortcuts, and he had yet to test his abilities and self-image against the realities of life.

At the same time, the problems facing Travis were complex and troubling enough to push even a resourceful adult to his spiritual and psychological limits. It was no accident that he began to romanticize his drinking days and recall with regret the pleasures of intoxication. Like many recovering alcoholics, he remained secretly convinced that only alcohol could make life worth living. As he reflected on the long, dry years ahead, he felt that by giving up alcohol he was burying one of his dearest and most dependable friends.

It should be obvious by now that simply *not drinking* will not keep a recovering alcoholic sober. If he does not quickly learn problem-solving skills, and if he continues to seek a quick fix to life's difficulties, he will almost inevitably return to his dependence upon alcohol or develop a new addiction to another drug. For the recovering alcoholic to remain sober, he must learn that it is unrealistic and dangerous to seek to live each day in a cloud of euphoria. He must also pay careful attention to the guidelines for recovery that have enabled other alcoholics to survive the pitfalls of sobriety.

23

Guidelines for Recovering Alcoholics

⌒

While serving in the U.S. Navy, I often heard that the book of safety regulations was written item by item as a result of the deaths of sailors—when a life was lost, a rule was born. The guidelines for recovering alcoholics have much the same history. Most are the result of years of experience, and they serve as beacons to direct recovering alcoholics to safe waters, while helping them avoid the dangerous shoals where so many have met disaster.

Many newly sober alcoholics are strongly tempted to think of themselves as exceptions to the rule, and those who love them should take care not to encourage this illusion. Most "exceptions" end up drinking again, and their failure to remain sober is usually directly related to their unwillingness to follow the example of other recovering alcoholics.

The following guidelines do not exhaust the wealth of information available to addicted drinkers in treatment programs and Alcoholics Anonymous, but they highlight some of the opportunities and dangers facing the newly sober alcoholic.

1. NEW PLAYGROUND, NEW PLAYMATES

It is all too easy for recovering alcoholics to walk out of a treatment center and into the arms of their former drinking buddies. The seductive nature of these relationships cannot be overemphasized. While teenagers are particularly susceptible to peer pressure, even grown adults may find themselves longing for the camaraderie and false sense of intimacy generated by shared intoxication.

Jeff was a friendly, outgoing, and desperately sick thirty-three-year-old when I met him in the intensive care unit. He had been admitted in an alcoholic coma and was bleeding so severely from his esophagus that I didn't expect him to live. His condition unexpectedly improved, and with very little resistance, he agreed to enter a treatment center. His family gave him a one-way ticket to a well-regarded program, but two weeks later he was back in Nashville, hanging out at his favorite bar. His drinking buddies had taken up a collection and sent him a bus ticket home. Tempted by the thought of old, familiar friends, Jeff accepted their offer, and the next time we met, he was again in the critical care unit. This time he was paralyzed from the waist down as a result of a drunk-driving accident.

Like Jeff, many alcoholics are involved in destructive relationships with people who try, consciously or unconsciously, to sabotage their sobriety. A husband, threatened by his wife's new sobriety, attempts to convince her that she is better company when she is drunk. A friend of a recovering alcoholic tries one too many times to pour him a drink. A colleague insists on sitting at a bar. Staying sober is the recovering alcoholic's number one priority, and, as much as circumstances allow, she must distance herself from people and relationships that undermine her recovery.

2. MAINTAIN AA ATTENDANCE

"I shouldn't have quit going to AA." It's the single most common expression I hear from relapsed alcoholics. In the excitement and euphoria of early recovery, it is easy for newly sober addicts to convince themselves that they, unlike other alcoholics, have no need for Alcoholics Anonymous. "I came out of a great treatment program on a real spiritual high," remembered one college student. "With God on my side, I didn't need AA and all that 'higher power' stuff. What could I learn from a bunch of old drunk people? Before I knew what hit me, I started drinking again. I went back to AA, and, little by little, I'm getting to where I want to be."

While it is true that some alcoholics stay sober without attending AA, thousands of men and women have died trying to prove that they should be included in this number. To ignore the program of Alcoholics Anonymous or to abandon it early in the recovery process is to throw away the most successful and time-tested support system available for recovering alcoholics.

3. EASY DOES IT

Through years of compulsive drinking, the recovering alcoholic has grown accustomed to instant gratification of her needs and desires. Sober, she may attempt to make up for lost time by trying to solve all her problems at once. She may be easily distracted by irrelevant issues, have an instant answer for every question, and be deeply discouraged when confronted with obstacles. "It's the alcoholics who try to set the world on fire who drink again," said Rachel, a recovering alcoholic. "If you don't learn patience, you're as good as gone. When I was drinking, I had to have everything yesterday. Now I know how to wait. And if I have to wait all my life for what I want, I will."

Family members, friends, colleagues, and faith leaders should likewise exercise caution in their expectations for the recovering alcoholic. Travis was appointed a leader in his church shortly after his first year of sobriety, and the burden of this responsibility played a significant role in the development of his second addiction. "If I had been more mature, I never would have accepted the position," he reflected. "But people's expectations were very high. Their confidence in me fed my pride and my need for instant gratification."

"Keep it simple," advises the Big Book of Alcoholics Anonymous. As much as possible, recovering alcoholics should avoid unnecessary complications, including, especially in the first year of their sobriety, dramatic changes in employment, marital status, or geographical location.

KEEP IT SIMPLE

When I began recovery, my brain was fried. I needed things real simple. I learned that the way to stay clean and sober was not to drink, no matter what. When I got scared or angry, I could kick or scream. I could even throw a bowl through the window. But the one thing I couldn't do was use drugs or alcohol.

—JENNIFER, age 28

---

4. AVOID MOOD-ALTERING DRUGS

Every year thousands of addicted drinkers like Travis inadvertently trigger their craving for alcohol by ingesting mood-altering drugs. Some fall victim to uninformed doctors who too freely write prescriptions for tranquilizers or pain pills. Others take weight loss pills, swallow cough syrup, or use a seemingly harmless decongestant. Because mood-altering drugs are interchangeable (the nerve endings in the brain that are created by addiction do not know the difference between Xanax and alcohol) and because many leading over-the-counter drugs contain alcohol, recovering alcoholics must be extraordinarily cautious in their use of medicine. *Before taking any medicine, recovering alcoholics must make a safety check with an informed doctor or addiction counselor.* Also, many recovering alcoholics, having accustomed themselves to taking medication for relatively minor physical and mental discomforts, have a low threshold for pain. Now they must learn to let some pain and discomfort run its course.

For their part, doctors must take greater care in prescribing medications. Several years ago, a patient came to me complaining of "nerves" and insomnia. Three years earlier, his nine-year-old son had been killed by a drunk driver, and the father had held him in his arms while he died. The man had never recovered from his grief, and now he needed help sleeping. I gave him a month's supply of sleeping pills, but only four days later his wife called my office for a refill. "My husband is acting just like he did when he was addicted to alcohol," she said with alarm. I immediately canceled the man's prescription. Fortunately no harm was done, but my oversight could easily have led to disaster.

A further word of caution is in order. The majority of alcoholics today are cross-addicted to one or more drugs—cocaine, marijuana, tranquilizers, hallucinogens, methamphetamines—and it is important that all recovering alcoholics understand that they cannot stay sober and continue to use other addictive substances. Many young alcoholics in particular try to convince themselves that they can abstain from alcohol and still occasionally use illegal, mood-altering drugs. Like most mood-altering prescription drugs, however, illegal drugs have the ability to mimic the effect of alcohol on the reward centers of the brain. And in almost every case, they lead the recovering alcoholic back to drinking within a few days or weeks.

5. IDENTIFY TRIGGERS

The changes in brain structure and function that create addictive craving are not temporary, and there is some research suggesting that they may last as long as life itself. As s result, recovering alcoholics are likely to have a permanent vulnerability to tastes, smells, sights, and sounds that trigger their craving for a drink. They are also vulnerable to emotional or behavioral triggers, such as anger, loneliness, fatigue, or a loss of confidence and self-esteem.

"Just like the first few grains of snow that start down a hillside trigger an avalanche, a relapse can be triggered by what seems like the smallest of events or emotions," reflected Andre Corley of the Sante Center for Healing.[1] Identifying these triggers and learning how to handle them is one of the most important parts of relapse prevention for any addicted drinker.

6. LEARN NEW WAYS OF COPING WITH EMOTIONAL PAIN

The depressant qualities of alcohol, combined with the drinker's own rationalization and denial, often effectively cut the alcoholic off from the pain of his addiction. After years of living with numbed and suppressed emotions, he may be caught off guard by the force of his painful feelings, including anger, sadness, embarrassment, anxiety, and resentment.

"This business of resentment is infinitely grave," explained the founder of Alcoholics Anonymous. "We found that it is fatal. For when harboring such feelings, we shut ourselves off from the sunlight of the Spirit. The insanity of alcohol returns and we drink again. And with us, to drink is to die."[2]

In the past, recovering alcoholics translated painful emotions of every stripe into "I need a drink." In recovery, they learn to accept a certain amount of emotional pain as a natural part of life, to separate their painful feelings from a desire to drink, and to find alternative methods for dealing with strong emotions. This education usually begins in treatment and continues with the 12-step program of AA.

RELEASING RESENTMENTS

I know of no better way for releasing recurring deep resentments than the path suggested in the Big Book of Alcoholics Anonymous. The recovering alcoholic, or anyone, makes a list of the people she resents, specifies their hurtful action, and identifies why she felt threatened by their behavior. She then makes a list of her own faults and fears, and honestly admits her wrongs to other people. After these admissions, she can more easily see those who have offended her as she sees herself: a person in need of tolerance, patience, and pity. The recovering alcoholic asks a Higher Power to give her this tolerance and kindness, and to show her a way that she can be helpful to the person who has wronged her.[3]

Eventually many, if not most, recovering alcoholics will find it helpful to consult a therapist or counselor. In a therapeutic setting, recovering alcoholics can find the courage and support they need to address their hidden wounds, including any childhood trauma. They can also learn new ways of communicating and coping with deep feelings and emotions. In choosing a therapist, it is important to find a professional who is:

- trained in substance abuse;
- empathic, supportive, and flexible; and
- not overly wedded to any one model of therapy.

A broad range of other research-based interventions are proving helpful to recovering alcoholics. These include EMDR (Eye Movement Desensitization and Reprocessing), meditation, yoga, physical therapy, sensory integration, and deep-breathing exercises.

Interestingly, there is now an identified acupuncture protocol that has been shown to improve an alcoholic's chances of recovery if it is used in conjunction with regular attendance at AA meetings.

A TENDER GRIEF

From the beginning, God has been in the business of taking what seems like tragedy and turning it into blessing. God did it in my life, and I have everything in the world to be grateful for. After drinking to oblivion almost every night for fifteen years, I sobered up with the help of AA.

Of course, the physical consequences of my addiction are still there. I've lost part of my stomach, and my memory and energy aren't what they were. All this once depressed me, but it doesn't concern me anymore. I should have been dead twenty years ago. God has restored to me so much more than I ever lost, and I know that every day I'm alive is a gift.

A few months ago, our nineteen-year-old son was killed in an automobile accident. I think it's true what they say: no one knows the pain of losing a child until it happens to them. But the miracle for me was that I could go through my son's death and the devastation I still feel without ever thinking of taking a drink. I used to get drunk if I had a flat tire. But God has made me a new person. In Alcoholics Anonymous, we call it "a spiritual awakening," a personality change at the deepest levels of life.

So I'm grateful I can be sober today. I am able to be a comfort and strength to my wife and children, and we are all going through this time of grief together. And although it's still hard to know my son is gone, I am sure beyond any question that he is with God, and I know that we will be together again.

—DAN, age 58

---

6. IF THE CRAVING RETURNS . . .

Six months, five years, or three decades after his last drink, it is possible for the recovering alcoholic to experience an apparently sudden and unexpected return of his physical craving for alcohol. By making a plan in advance and taking immediate action, the addicted drinker can prevent a full-blown relapse. The following are essential steps:

- Don't pretend the craving isn't there, and don't underestimate its power.

- Seek professional help and increase AA attendance.

- Talk over the experience with other recovering alcoholics.

- Avoid triggers. Normally recovering alcoholics can attend restaurants and parties where alcohol is served, but during this vulnerable time it may be best to avoid places where alcohol is readily available.

- Under the direction of a physician, take prescription drugs that reduce craving and/or reduce the pleasure of drinking. Two drugs that have been shown to reduce craving are naltrexone and acamprosate. Antabuse, an older drug that interacts with alcohol to make the drinker violently ill, can also be very effective.[4]

For recovering alcoholics who take proper precautions, attend AA, practice the Twelve Steps, and seek professional help when necessary, there is the joyous prospect of living alcohol-free for the rest of their lives. If their family members and close friends are to join in this celebration of sobriety, it is essential that they, too, recognize their need for help and commit themselves to a recovery program.

24

Family Recovery

~

When Joel returned to his synagogue after twenty years of estrangement caused in large part by his addictive drinking, he was greeted with open arms. He and his wife, Beth, became enthusiastic supporters of the temple, and they began to observe for the first time the traditions of their faith.

Over time, their rabbi noticed that Beth was becoming increasingly depressed and withdrawn. "No one knows what it's like for me," she told him one day. "My husband ruined our family by drinking away our money, and I'm left to pick up the pieces. Everyone thinks he's so terrific, but they don't have to live with his mistakes."

The rabbi urged Beth to forgive her husband and get on with her life. Unknown to him, Beth herself was already drinking heavily, and she had just begun an affair with another addicted drinker in the congregation. "After a lot of heartache, Beth finally went into treatment," recalled her rabbi. "But she had far more difficulty giving up alcohol than her husband, and they are now divorced. As far as I know, while her husband is sober, Beth is still drinking."

"At the time, I didn't know anything about the family dynamics of addiction," added the rabbi. "As a congregation, we heaped attention on Beth's husband, with good results. But we didn't recognize that she needed help too. She had been through hell, living with an addict, but we didn't notice her deep pain until it took the form of addiction. Unfortunately, by that time, it was too late."

One of the most resilient myths of addiction is the belief that when the alcoholic stops drinking, his family's problems will disappear. Unfortunately, unhealthy family patterns that have taken years to develop are likely to persist through the early recovery period and, as in the case of Joel and Beth, may even worsen. If these problems remain unaddressed, they threaten the permanence of family bonds and can contribute to the alcoholic's decision to return to drinking.

The emotional dilemmas facing families in recovery follow a familiar pattern. They are happy that the alcoholic is sober but live in fear that, at any moment, he will begin drinking again. If he comes home late, they wonder if he has been out drinking. If he's depressed or angry, they worry that they have done something to cause a relapse. Old habits of communication die hard, and family members may fall back on familiar practices of criticism, defensiveness, and manipulation. They may resent the alcoholic for creating a new life, even as they, the innocent victims, struggle to deal with deep and abiding wounds.

The recovering alcoholic, meanwhile, is likely to be preoccupied with himself and his recovery. He may spend his free time going to meetings and hanging out with new friends instead of paying attention to his family. He may speak in "recovery jargon," and develop a new identity that aggravates the insecurities and resentments of his marriage partner.

In facing these difficulties, family members can be comforted by the knowledge that the transition period will not last forever and that they, too, can find the resources and tools they need for their own recovery process. This recovery does not depend on the alcoholic, and even if he or she never permanently stops drinking, family members can find new, more productive, and happier lives for themselves.

As families progress through the recovery process, the following steps will prove helpful.

STEP 1: FIND (PROFESSIONAL) HELP

Family members of alcoholics have often spent years ignoring their own physical, psychological, and spiritual well-being. To focus on themselves and move beyond unhealthy patterns of behavior, they most often need professional help, not just as individuals but as a family unit. This help is available from:

- counselors and therapists trained in both addiction and family dynamics;

- Al-Anon, Alateen, and ACOA (for adult children of alcoholics);

- other community groups, including university research programs.

A growing body of research confirms that family members benefit from cognitive and behavior skills training, 12-step programs, and the empathy and support of trained therapists. Ideally, family members have access to all three of these supports, but those who cannot find or afford professional assistance can still attend Al-Anon and Alateen and work their own 12-step program.

Children and adult children of alcoholics, who normally have developed high levels of self-reliance as a survival tool, may find it particularly difficult to seek professional assistance or attend a self-help group. Friends and family members can help by being patient and persistent, and by identifying and providing contact information for qualified professionals. A helpful book for professionals and anyone concerned for a recovering alcoholic is *The Alcoholic Family in Recovery: A Developmental Model*, by Stephanie Brown and Virginia Lewis (New York: Guilford Press, 1999).

Note: Like alcoholics, family members of addicted drinkers may have severe and high levels of trauma in their past. Professional assistance is needed to identify the trauma, to determine its developmental impact, and to provide appropriate treatment. Fortunately, the field of trauma treatment is rapidly progressing, and new research-based methods like EMDR (Eye Movement Desensitization and Reprocessing) are proving effective in enabling trauma survivors to find healing from potentially life-destroying events.

STEP 2: AVOID UNREALISTIC EXPECTATIONS OF THE RECOVERING ALCOHOLIC—AND ONE ANOTHER

High expectations and subsequent disappointments are a common trap for family members. In the early months of recovery, family members often swing back and forth between optimism and pessimism as they adjust their hopes and fears to the daily realities of living with a recovering alcoholic. They may find that, even sober, the recovering alcoholic is still a difficult person with whom to live. Indeed, he may be more touchy and irritable than ever, and it may be months or even years before he is capable of consistent and mature adult behavior.

In this potentially tumultuous time, family members, too, benefit from the basic insights of AA: take one day at a time, keep things simple, set realistic goals, and stay focused on one's own emotional and spiritual growth. It is helpful to remember that Al-Anon and professional counselors are not a cure-all for family problems. Rather, they are effective resources for family members as they work through the challenges of their own recovery process.

LETTING GO: A MOTHER'S STORY

While my daughter was addicted, I let things drift. I became spiritually barren, and I felt guilty and afraid all the time. Even after she began her recovery, I had panic spells. At night I was attacked by ominous, free-floating anxiety: it seemed as if at any moment something I hadn't counted on could come from out of nowhere to grab my child and drag her under.

But I've learned to let go and to trust God. Sometimes I can't believe all the things I've been able to surrender to God's care. I've given up trying to fix things for my daughter, and I've stopped always trying to make peace between family members. I've learned to let them work out their own problems. And through it all my daughter is like a flower that has opened up. She was closed up tight for so many years that we forgot what a wonderful human being was trapped inside. Now, she can give love and receive it, and she has blossomed into a beautiful young woman.

—DELORES
Mother of a young adult alcoholic

STEP 3: LEARN NEW WAYS TO COMMUNICATE

After years of living with an alcoholic, most family members have little understanding of the principles that govern good adult communication. They have spent too many years using words to attack or defend. Now they must learn, or relearn, the art of plain speaking. For most families, this process will require time and, when available and affordable, the help of a family therapist or other professional counselor.

If the alcoholic's emotional stability permits, at some point the family may choose, with the help of a professional counselor, to explain to the alcoholic what their life was like when he was drinking. If they can tell their story and express their feelings—grief, sadness, anger, hurt, shame, guilt, etc.—in a direct and nonjudgmental manner, the addicted drinker may come to a new understanding of the pain his family has experienced. Equipped with this common understanding, both the alcoholic and his family members can acknowledge the ways they have hurt one another, and they can move toward the forgiveness that leads to true restoration in relationships.

STEP 4: FREEDOM TO FORGIVE: A WORK IN PROGRESS

For most people, surrendering the past includes some form of forgiveness. The healing power of forgiveness is supported by numerous studies, but the act of forgiving those who have hurt us is a bit more complicated. It is a highly personal, often elusive, and profoundly spiritual power. No one is entitled to demand forgiveness from us, and yet when we are finally able to give forgiveness as a free gift, it has an extraordinary power to set us free.

"How much rental space are you willing to give to the people who hurt you?" is a question we ask impaired physicians in the Center for Professional Health at Vanderbilt University Medical Center. Over time, many of these recovering doctors are able to let go of the grief, anger, and resentment that have taken root inside. In the process, they find themselves freeing up space in their hearts for a more creative, productive, and grace-filled life.

When family members follow their own program of healing, they not only help themselves, but they increase the alcoholic's chances of achieving long-term sobriety. At the same time, many addicted drinkers have one or more relapses before becoming permanently sober. For this reason, it is important that both the alcoholic and her family members know how to recognize and respond to the symptoms of relapse.

SURRENDERING THE PAST: KATE'S STORY

Kate was eleven when her alcoholic father died from cirrhosis of the liver. Her mother plunged into a deep depression. She tormented her daughter with unpredictable and violent behavior, including physical abuse, screaming fits, false accusations, and days of morbid silence. When she began tearing up Kate's homework assignments, Kate learned to study outdoors on the street. Despite these hardships, Kate was an outstanding student. Her dream of a college education died when her mother became bedridden, and Kate was forced to go to work.

In her early thirties, Kate married and had four children. She was a reliable, disciplined person who never lost self-control, and over time she took on more and more family and community responsibilities. She was outwardly congenial, but inwardly she resented and envied friends who were more carefree and spontaneous.

"When you grow up without responsible parents, there's no order in your life," Kate said. "I had to make my own order, and I was deeply afraid of losing my hard-earned self-control.

"My memory of crying as a teenager was a wrenching shaking of my whole being," Kate added. "I thought if I let my guard down, even for a minute, I would completely fall apart."

Kate's turning point came after an automobile accident in which she was seriously injured. She was helped by a passerby, an exceptionally kind young man. Several weeks later, she learned that her rescuer had drowned in a boating accident because he was wearing hip boots that filled up with water.

"I felt God spoke to me about those boots," remembered Kate. "I saw myself as a small child walking through a swampy forest, wearing hip boots for protection. But then I was in a boat, and God was telling me to take the boots off, that I didn't need them anymore. They had been protection, but now they were dangerous. If I kept them on and a storm arose, I would drown."

For Kate, it was a moment of remarkable insight into her troubled past. "When I was a child, my life really was a swamp," she said. "I needed to be self-sufficient and controlling. Even learning how to manipulate people was a matter of survival. But now my life was different. I wasn't on my own, and I had outer and inner strengths that weren't available to me as a child.

"I came to understand that those hip boots were from God, but they were only useful for a time," added Kate. "They didn't serve a purpose anymore, and if I didn't get rid of them, they would drag me under."

For family members of an alcoholic, the surrender of old defense mechanisms, hurtful memories, anger, and resentment is an essential but often complicated step toward spiritual and mental health. Such surrender rarely takes place in a single moment, but is rather a long-term process. "Even now I have to consciously commit myself to not trying to control and manipulate others," said Kate. "It's hard to give up behavior that worked so well for so many years, and I'm still not totally free from it. But day by day I'm learning to live in a more honest and vulnerable way."

25

Relapse Prevention

~

Evelyn was an influential member of a government task force on alcoholism. As a recovering alcoholic, she attended AA meetings on a daily basis and was a frequent speaker at national and international conferences on addiction. Her work brought her into daily contact with the rich and powerful, and she helped a number of well-known politicians with their drinking problems.

As Evelyn's reputation grew, her behavior with her colleagues and friends deteriorated. She became increasingly opinionated and dictatorial and broke off relationships at the slightest provocation. Because of her travel schedule, she seldom attended AA meetings unless she was invited to speak.

One night, while flying home from a conference, Evelyn ordered a cocktail. It was only an experiment. For years she had heard "it's the first drink that gets you drunk," but now she felt certain that she had been sober long enough to handle one drink. Evelyn was right—one drink was all that she wanted. Elated, she decided that, as long as she wasn't with other recovering alcoholics, she would enjoy an occasional drink.

For more than a year, Evelyn drank socially and slowly fell back into addictive drinking. One drink became two, two turned into three, and eventually she was rushing home from work every evening for a glass of wine. Too ashamed to ask for help, she plunged into a deep depression and began to plan her own death.

With the help of a concerned friend and despite her own embarrassment, Evelyn entered a treatment center where she had directed dozens of other alcoholics. By then she was hearing voices urging her to kill herself, and she suffered a complete mental breakdown. It was only after many months of hospitalization that she was able to gradually regain her sanity and her sobriety.

SLOW SLIDE INTO FREE FALL

Like Evelyn, the vast majority of recovering alcoholics who begin to drink again are not caught off guard by a sudden craving for alcohol but by a slow slide into careless thinking and living. They come to believe that they can drink like other people, and this belief tempts them into trying just one drink. Some, like Evelyn, are able to control their drinking for an extended time, but sooner or later, they slide back into addictive drinking.

However slowly an alcoholic loses control, once a relapse is fully under way, it has an internal power that can bring an alcoholic to the point of death in a matter of weeks. Perhaps because of permanent changes in the brain's reward system, the physical adjustments that the body once made to adapt itself to the constant presence of alcohol can be re-created almost instantly. Even after years of abstinence, life-threatening withdrawal symptoms may reappear in less than a day.

Crippling feelings of anxiety, guilt, and self-hatred may also come back with intensity, and the recovering alcoholic rapidly returns to rationalizing and denying his drinking problem. He falls into old patterns of behavior with his family, friends, and colleagues, and in many cases his addiction appears to progress faster than ever.

Maria was an alcoholism counselor who had been sober for twenty years when she met and married a prosperous building contractor. One night shortly after her wedding, Maria's husband took her out to dinner and urged her to try a drink. Eager to please, Maria ordered a gin and tonic. Within a week, Maria was drinking a gallon of gin a day, and by the end of the second week, she was in our critical care unit, nearly dead from alcoholic hepatitis. Maria was in a far more advanced stage of alcoholism than when she quit drinking twenty years earlier, and she never completely recovered from the acute physical damage caused by her relapse.

PREVENTING RELAPSE

Recovery from addiction, as we have seen, is not merely a matter of abstinence but a commitment to sobriety, a lifelong journey toward physical, emotional, social, and spiritual healing. Perhaps because of the complexity of this journey, relapse, particularly in the first five years of sobriety, is a normal part of recovery. If treated properly, it can become an important step toward sober living.

At the same time, relapse is not inevitable and it *is* dangerous. "I know that I have another drunk left in me," say many recovering alcoholics. "I just don't know if I have another recovery." For the recovering alcoholic, it is far easier to avoid triggers and deal with the symptoms of an impending relapse than to pick up the pieces after a return to addictive drinking.

Most recovering alcoholics, like Evelyn, signal their approaching relapse by adopting "dry drunk" behavior. They may become impatient, easily bored, resentful, judgmental, and full of grandiose ideas. They may overreact to minor difficulties, and become as rigid and thoughtless as they were in their drinking days. They are often unusually depressed or euphoric, and they may begin once again to blame others for their own shortcomings.

To avoid this slide back into addictive drinking, it is important that recovering alcoholics participate in an ongoing recovery program. For most people, this means ongoing AA attendance and actively working the Twelve Steps. "All those years I was in AA, I was an agnostic," Evelyn reflected. "Although I recommended the Twelve Steps to others, I never practiced them myself. I thought I was doing great without them; instead I was setting myself up for a relapse.

"Today, I am convinced that these steps are God's invitation to a transformed life for people who suffer from addiction. I still stumble and fall, but day by day, I see important changes. And I face most days with serenity, confident that in the end my life is in the hands of a loving and merciful God."

The sobriety of recovering alcoholics is also substantially strengthened by:

- training to recognize the symptoms of relapse;

- taking a periodic inventory of attitudes and behavior, preferably with the help of a spouse, close friend, counselor, or spiritual advisor;

- taking appropriate medications, when needed, to alleviate craving and to discourage drinking.

Coping with the possibility of a relapse, like most of life, is a delicate balancing act. Recovering alcoholics need not live in fear of a return to addictive drinking—an alcoholic who is afraid of relapse may begin drinking to overcome his chronic anxiety. At the same time, it is important to have a healthy appreciation for the power of addiction and the permanence of the alcoholic's vulnerability.

Terence T. Gorski, a pioneer in "relapse prevention therapy," has developed a useful tool for recovering alcoholics and family members to identify symptoms of relapse. This comprehensive questionnaire, AWARE, can be found on the Internet, and studies confirm that it is a reliable and valid predictor of alcoholism relapse. Go to: www.tgorski.com/relapse/Aware_Relapse_Questionaire.pdf.

SCIENCE AND AA

For years, members of AA have taught one another that "one drink is too many, and a thousand drinks are not enough." Now, breakthroughs in medical research may explain the biomedical foundation for this insight. Chronic alcohol use changes the brain's reward system by, perversely, dampening the pleasurable effects of alcohol and increasing the alcoholic's craving for alcohol. The alcoholic's intense craving is in part a result of the permanent increase in "alcohol-sensitive" buds on the brain's neurons—a potentially lifelong change in brain structure and function.[1]

WHAT IF THE RECOVERING ALCOHOLIC DRINKS AGAIN?

Because of the speed at which addiction progresses after relapse, it is important that families, friends, and colleagues act immediately if they discover that the recovering alcoholic has returned to drinking. Some relapsing drinkers will ask for help; otherwise, family members should seek professional counsel and consider a second group intervention.

Family members can encourage the relapsing alcoholic to return to treatment or to attend ninety meetings of Alcoholics Anonymous in ninety days. More treatment centers are recognizing that relapse is a normal part of recovery, and some insurance companies cover additional outpatient or even inpatient treatment. In my own medical practice, I recommend that recovering alcoholics who have had one or more relapses commit themselves to lifelong participation in AA.

Note: It is important that family members and friends not panic during relapse and that they avoid falling back into old behavior patterns. Every chronic illness tends toward relapse, and family members and friends should resist the temptation to berate the alcoholic or portray relapse as a personal failing. Rather, they can support the relapsed drinker in her effort to become aware of the behavior and attitudes that led to relapse. They can also support her efforts to make lifestyle adjustments that reduce the likelihood of another relapse.

TURNING POINT

I was addicted to alcohol and drugs for twenty-eight years. In the early days of my recovery, I cleaned homes, and this became a turning point for me.

Some of the people I worked for kept alcohol in their cupboards, and one day I realized that it wasn't going to jump out and attack me. Alcohol didn't have magical powers. In fact, unless I made a conscious choice to put it in my system, it didn't have any power at all.

—SYLVIA, age 45

MULTIPLE RELAPSES

Some alcoholics have repeated relapses before becoming permanently sober, and family members and friends should not give up on a drinker just because he is having difficulty maintaining his sobriety. One of my good friends was in and out of Alcoholics Anonymous seven times in six years before he was finally able to quit drinking. Many others have two or three relapses before becoming permanently sober.

In the presence of repeated relapses, it is wise to consider prolonged inpatient treatment, if it is available and affordable. It is also helpful to focus on the success of periods of sobriety, rather than the acute pain of relapse. One alcoholism counselor reflected:

> I had a young patient who was addicted to alcohol, heroin, and tranquilizers. When I first met Jane she was getting high every day. After treatment, she was clean for eight months. She slipped, came back, and was drug-free for another fourteen months. Then she went on a drinking binge. Now it's been over two years that she's been without a drink or any other drug.
>
> A few months ago, she experienced a crushing disappointment when she learned that she no longer had the mental aptitude to fulfill her lifelong ambition to be a journalist. She weathered this crisis without resorting to drugs. Although in terms of recovery statistics, Jane's repeated relapses make her a failure, in my own eyes and in her own, she is a remarkable success.

One final word of warning: there are millions of recovering alcoholics in our world, and most of them choose to remain anonymous. They are our friends, our colleagues, fellow members of our churches, synagogues, mosques, and temples. What they need from us is support, not temptation. For example, Angela is a recovering alcoholic and a nurse working in a hospice for terminally ill patients. One night after a particularly bad week, her hospital chaplain encouraged the entire staff to unwind with a bottle of champagne. Angela, not wanting to reject his gift, took one drink, and then four more. For two weeks, she was engaged in a minute-by-minute battle with her craving for alcohol, and it was only by going back to a treatment center that she was able to return to sobriety.

Because it is widely considered a friendly and hospitable gesture to urge alcohol on friends and guests, we must all take care that we do not, unawares, create a serious problem for a recovering alcoholic. We can honor the struggle of addicted drinkers by making the conscious commitment to never pressure other people to drink.

26

What If the Alcoholic Never Stops Drinking?

~

Billie Jean realized that her husband was an alcoholic the night her third child was born. "I asked Don to take care of our two small children while I was in the hospital," she said. "He loved them very much, but he got drunk anyway, and I knew he was no longer in control of his drinking."

For the next twenty years, Billie Jean adjusted her life to make room for an alcoholic husband. She stopped inviting friends home, became both father and mother to her children, and accepted without complaining her husband's unchanging daily routine of working, drinking, and sleeping. Don was never physically violent, but no one in the family was spared from his cruel verbal abuse.

"Living in an environment of unrelenting criticism and constant accusation is like the slow dripping of water on a rock," remembered Billie Jean. "Eventually, even strong people get worn down. But I wasn't a strong person. I grew up wanting to please everyone, and I idolized my husband. I wanted him to love me, and I gradually let him take more and more control of my life.

"When I saw how much he was hurting the children, I thought

of leaving him, but I was too emotionally and financially dependent to be on my own. I didn't think I could support myself and the kids, and even though Don was drunk most of the time, I couldn't imagine life without him."

Shortly after her last child left home, Billie Jean began to seek a deeper relationship with God, and, with the help of church friends, she found a new sense of security and self-worth. Don was disturbed by the changes in Billie Jean's behavior, and he stepped up his efforts to control their relationship. "He decided to move us to a new town," Billie Jean remembered. "I didn't have the courage to say no, so I went with him. Away from old friends and our family, Don was the only person in my life.

"My old feelings of dependency returned, but there wasn't anything to depend on," added Billie Jean. "I was exhausted by the effort of living with Don's unpredictable anger and constant negativity. There was a strong sense of evil in our house, and I was always afraid of what he might do next. Finally he went to a doctor for liver problems, but he refused to get help for his drinking. I lost hope that he would ever get better."

Within a year, Billie Jean packed up and left her husband. She was fifty-two years old, she had no college diploma or prior work experience, and she was without any means of financial support. "It was my spiritual life and the support of friends that gave me confidence to make a move," Billie Jean recalled. "I felt that God provided for the details of my life—a place to live, a job, good friends—and I was always conscious of God's presence and sustaining love."

Today, Billie Jean has completed college and graduate school, and she is teaching in a community college. Her husband is still drinking, and in eight years she has never returned to her former home. "Sometimes people in my church encourage me to return to my marriage," she reflected, "But I think they would be less eager for me to return if they knew what a miracle it was that I was finally able to leave."

It is a sad and disturbing truth that some addicted drinkers persistently refuse help and give no sign of ever recovering from their addiction. In these circumstances, family members, close friends, and colleagues must make hard personal decisions about their future relationship with the alcoholic. Although there are no simple rules that apply to every situation, it is helpful to keep in mind the following points:

1. *Family members should not continue to live with a physically violent alcoholic.* Although violent family dynamics are always complicated and dangerous, there are community resources for the protection of battered spouses and their children. With professional assistance and police protection if necessary, family members who experience physical battering should remove themselves from the alcoholic's presence as soon as they are able to safely do so.

2. *Verbal abuse and unpredictable cruel behavior can be even more damaging than physical violence.* When the alcoholic becomes a psychological and spiritual threat to her family, it is time for a separation. This separation should not end until the alcoholic quits drinking. Husbands and wives will most often need the help of faith leaders and other professional helpers to make individual decisions concerning legal actions and divorce.

3. *Money is a great weapon.* People who are financially dependent upon a drinking alcoholic should begin to prepare themselves to be self-supporting, even if they do not plan to leave the alcoholic. One of my patients stayed with her drinking husband long enough to get a business degree and find full-time employment and then left to protect herself and her children from further physical and emotional damage.

4. *Family members and friends must be patient with wives or husbands who regularly leave their alcoholic spouses only to return*

within a few weeks or months to an unchanged situation. Particularly in cases of physical and/or emotional abuse, many spouses often leave and return several times before they are able to make a final separation. During this time, they need continuous, nonjudgmental support from their friends. Even though their indecision and unpredictability may tax the patience of those who love them, it is important to understand that repeated coming and going may be a natural part of the separation process.

5. *Husbands and wives who have left alcoholic marriages should not be counseled to return to them while the alcoholic is still drinking.* Only a very few people in special circumstances are able to live with a drinking alcoholic and not experience profound psychological and/or physical damage. A "marriage at all cost" attitude is unrealistic and dangerous.

6. *Churches, synagogues, and other faith communities must take seriously their pastoral role for people whose marriages and families fall apart because of addiction.* These individuals need the same sympathy and compassion, and time for mourning, that is given to families during times of death. They may have internalized the alcoholic's accusations, and they may be burdened with crippling feelings of guilt. Faith leaders can help by assuring family members that they are not responsible for the alcoholic's continued drinking and that no one can cause or cure another's addiction. Words of consolation should be reinforced with a message of hope: the alcoholic may yet stop drinking, but regardless of his or her path, family members, as individuals and as a unit, can claim their own productive and happy future.

27

A Call to Action

~

Sometimes it takes a community to bring a person to healing.
—LORETTA TATE, Community Activist
Washington, D.C.

In many ways it was like any other AA meeting. I sat in an uncomfortable chair in a crowded room and listened to a middle-aged man tell his personal story of loss and redemption: heavy drinking at an early age; loss of physical and mental health; family breakup; finally, with the help of a friend and AA, sobriety.

The year was 2001, and I was in a country outside the United States. The speaker was a computer programmer who had spent years as an addicted drinker. His story was unremarkable in all but one chilling detail: his job. During all the years he was seriously impaired by alcohol, he was monitoring his country's nuclear arsenal and supervising its first-strike capacity.

For me, it was a stark and unnerving reminder that the world is increasingly one enormous village—with a terrible drinking problem. "The human race—with all its distinct ethnic tongues, foods, customs and prejudices—is moving closer to one address," reflected an observer. "Call it www.earth."[1]

EXPANDING MARKETS

On this fragile planet, we have a remarkable opportunity for social and spiritual advancement through sober, transformative living. But the quality of life we share together in the years ahead will depend in no small degree on how we address the social problems caused by alcohol abuse and addiction.

These problems are aggravated by the worldwide reach of the alcohol industry, which spends some $2 billion annually in advertising. Many of their most persuasive messages are aimed at groups who can least afford the high price tags of abuse and addiction. Their targets include:

- women and young people;
- members of the emerging middle class in developing countries;
- the countries and satellites that made up the former Soviet Union.

Ironically, developing countries are increasing their imports of alcohol, and members of the emerging middle class in poor countries continue to fall back into poverty because of alcohol abuse and addiction.

In the United States, where affluence and materialism create problems of their own, sports and entertainment figures bombard television viewers with the message that drinking is the ticket to success, happiness, and the good life. "If you can manage to get some of the powers of the liquor industry talking off the record," said one prominent alcoholism researcher, "they will tell you that they never sell alcohol; they really sell sex and sophistication. The alcohol is merely a subliminal partner . . . Children pick up these signals. That's education."[2]

This education is reinforced by the remarkable amount of free publicity received by the alcohol industry through magazine stories, comic books, newspaper articles, and most importantly, movies and television. One study of popular TV shows revealed that, while smoking incidents have remarkably decreased, an average of more than eight drinks of alcohol are taken per television hour.[3] Authorities agree that this constant flow of alcohol results in the "normalization" of drinking. It becomes understood by our children and throughout our society that the consumption of alcoholic beverages is necessary to lead a satisfying life.

BUILDING FENCES

Working with alcoholics and their families is much like standing at the base of a cliff, picking up the bodies of victims who have fallen over the edge. We can only work there so long before we begin to think about climbing to the top and building a fence to prevent people from wandering too close to the edge.

As individuals, faith groups, and voluntary associations, there are any number of fence-building steps we can take to help address our society's drinking problem. One of the most basic steps, however, is to examine our personal drinking habits and make a conscious decision to drink moderately or not at all.

RESPONSIBLE DRINKING: MODERATION OR ABSTINENCE

Individual attitudes toward drinking alcohol are largely determined by family, religious, and community-wide values. These values often change over time, and, in the face of modern corporate advertising, many people of faith find it increasingly difficult to maintain their values and pass them on to their children.

I am aware that in my own Judeo-Christian faith tradition, there have been, and remain, widely divergent views toward alcoholic beverages. Both the Torah and the Bible have passages that support moderate drinking, and in more recent American history, even the much-maligned Puritans viewed wine as a gift from God "that gladdens the heart of man." (Psalm 104:15).

In contrast, by the late nineteenth and early twentieth centuries in the United States and Great Britain, faith leaders and social reformers identified alcohol abuse and alcoholism as the major cause of widespread, intergenerational poverty. In these years, Americans were spending more than a billion dollars a year on alcoholic beverages—compared to $200 million for public education. The primary victims of high alcoholism rates were women and children without legal protection from domestic violence. At the same time, most political meetings were held in saloons, which women were not allowed to enter.

For these reasons, liberals and conservatives alike hailed the passage of the Prohibition Amendment in 1919. In his funeral address for "John Barleycorn," the revivalist Billy Sunday spoke for many:

> Goodbye John. The reign of tears is over. The slums will soon
> be only a memory. We will turn our prisons into factories and
> our jails into storehouses and corncribs. Men will walk upright
> now, women will smile, and the children will laugh. Hell will
> be forever for rent.[4]

This euphoria was short-lived. Despite Prohibition's success in lowering the incidence of alcoholism and alcohol-related problems, it had enormous drawbacks, including opening the door for organized crime to take over the production and distribution of alcohol.[5] Today, moderate drinking is acceptable to many, if not most, American cultural groups. Recent studies have also demonstrated that moderate drinking of red wine lowers cholesterol levels and decreases the rate of heart attack and stroke.

As a medical doctor working in the field of alcohol addiction, I believe that moderate drinking—defined by health experts as no more than two drinks per day for men and one drink for women—is a sensible and responsible choice for many people. At the same time, I think there are compelling reasons why many of us should give abstinence serious consideration.

WEDDING PARTY

[Looking at the family photo album] we paused at the portrait of a wedding party and were stunned by who was missing. Uncle Ray died in a drunk-driving accident; cousin Sophie was far away, strung out on drugs. Grandma had just died. At the time, we thought it was a stroke. Really, she had fallen down the stairs, drunk, and died from a head injury. Staring at that picture, the damage and the losses from generations of alcoholism stood out . . . Then we looked around at each other—who was here today and who was sober? We've come a long way.

—From *The Alcoholic Family in Recovery:*
A Developmental Model[6]

First, it is my view that anyone with evidence of addiction in their family tree—grandparents, uncles, aunts, fathers, mothers, brothers, sisters—should avoid drinking alcohol. They may have inherited a significant genetic susceptibility to addiction, and the rewards of drinking do not balance out the risks. Recently, a man who descended from four generations of alcoholics asked me if that meant he would have to give up even an occasional beer with the boys. I had to tell him, "That's exactly what it means." In the presence of a family history of addiction, all drinking becomes high-risk drinking.

Second, despite the pronounced role of heredity, there is no way to predict who will or will not become an alcoholic. What we do know is that one out of ten social drinkers will become alcoholics, and that the majority of these will drift into addiction *unconsciously*. Given the odds, many people may understandably conclude that an ounce of prevention is worth a pound of cure and decide to forgo drinking alcohol.

Finally, all of us need to consider seriously the effect that alcohol has on the part of our brains that controls inhibitions. Even when we are at our best, when our inhibitions are in full force, we may be susceptible to certain temptations and our own character weaknesses. If we find that alcohol has become a partner to unhealthy behaviors and rituals—heavy drinking, gambling, pornography, sexual addiction, etc.—we may want to consider abstinence as part of our commitment to, and search for, mental and spiritual health.

TEMPERATE TEMPERANCE

A word of warning about efforts to alert young people to the dangers of alcohol: *scare tactics are notoriously ineffective.* Rigid attitudes and dogmatic approaches undermine credibility and usually result in teenagers dismissing the information they receive. This natural and healthy rebellion against manipulation may be one reason that children of dogmatic teetotalers are thought to be at higher risk for developing alcohol addiction than their peers from more moderate families.[7]

Mark Twain's advice is well taken: "Temperate temperance is best. Intemperate temperance injures the cause of temperance." The best way to talk with children and adults about alcohol is to give them information in an objective and nonalarmist fashion, and to equip them with social skills for resisting peer pressure. The "Letter to Grandchildren" in Appendix A is one example of a nonalarmist, factual approach to young people with a family history of addiction.

A CENTRAL ROLE FOR FAITH GROUPS

Faith groups in particular are in a position to play a central role in community recovery efforts. With a small investment of time and effort, any church, synagogue, mosque, temple, or other worshipping community can offer help to alcoholics and their families. First steps include:

1. *Identify Resource People.* Every worshipping community will benefit from having a core of people who care about alcohol and drug addiction. This group ideally includes, among others, recovering alcoholics/drug addicts and substance abuse professionals.

2. *Educate the Congregation.* Faith leaders can help their congregations understand the dangers of addiction and the importance of treatment through sermons, workshops, short talks, and the study of sacred texts. A poll of my own denomination showed that, although 83 percent of ministers believed that the church should address alcohol abuse, more than 70 percent had never preached a sermon on the subject.[8] This silence may spring from an understandable desire to avoid identification with strident antidrinking groups, but faith leaders must find creative and persuasive ways to talk to their communities about alcohol and drug abuse.

3. *Encourage Compassion.* Nadia, whose story we heard in Chapter 2, belongs to a small church group that meets every week for two hours of Bible study and intimate conversation. Even after five years in the group, Nadia has never told anyone she is a recovering alcoholic.

"I've heard them talk about alcoholics," Nadia said. "I know what they would think of me if I said I had the same problem. For the sake of our friendships, I keep this part of my life a secret." Nadia, ironically, is one of two recovering alcoholics in the group; another woman has also chosen to keep silent for fear of rejection.

Sadly, such fears are well founded. Studies show that people with strong religious convictions have harsher attitudes toward alcoholics than those for whom religion is completely unimportant.[9] In my own religious tradition, many recovering alcoholics I know refuse to attend church because of their memories of the condemning attitude of their fellow Christians.

"Everyone in this world is some kind of weakling," said the late Reverend Sam Shoemaker, addressing a group of recovering alcoholics. "If he thinks he is not, then pride is his weakness, and it is the greatest weakness of all." The basis of spiritual unity, Shoemaker added, is our common need for forgiveness and healing.[10]

THE POWER OF FAITH

Religion, in ways that we appreciate but do not understand, provides forgiveness of sins and relief from guilt. Unlike many intractable habits that others find merely annoying, alcoholism inflicts enormous pain and injury on those around the alcoholic. As a result the alcoholic, already demoralized by his inability to stop drinking, experiences almost insurmountable guilt from the torture he has inflicted on others. In such an instance, absolution becomes an important part of the healing process.[11]

—GEORGE E. VAILLANT
Professor of Psychiatry, Harvard Medical School

Faith groups have a vital role to play in addressing the spiritual needs of addicted drinkers and drug addicts. The guilt and shame felt by addicts who have grown up in vibrant faith traditions is even more pronounced than that of their secular counterparts. Often, long after they stop drinking, they fear that God has permanently rejected them. Their fellow believers can offer them the assurance of God's love and forgiveness.

Many faith groups support recovering addicts by providing meeting space to AA, NA (Narcotics Anonymous), Al-Anon, ACOA (Adult Children of Alcoholics), and other 12-step groups. They also can provide the vision and staying power to play a major role in community prevention efforts, including advocating for community-wide, comprehensive public-health strategies to address substance abuse. Smaller but effective interventions include moving liquor stores away from proximity to schools, raising taxes on alcohol to price it out of reach of young people, and advocating for research-based school intervention and prevention programs.

For most of us, our most effective action may be to teach ourselves and our children to celebrate life's goodness and cope with its difficulties without resorting to heavy drinking or drug abuse. As contemporary culture becomes increasingly devoted to the pursuit of pleasure, and as we become more accustomed to instant relief from pain, we must reaffirm our commitment to live joyful, productive, and sober lives.

PREVENTION WISDOM

- By itself, information about the dangers of drugs and alcohol . . . has little or no effect on use.

- Short-term approaches—one-shot presentations on alcohol and drugs—are ineffective. Students need to be provided with consistent, extended drug education programs.

- Programs that do impact young people's drug use are those that teach skills for resisting influences to use alcohol and other drugs and that help young people develop strong norms against use. The effects of even these programs, however, often dissipate after two or three years.

- School-based programs that have shown more lasting effects on drug and alcohol use have either offered booster sessions or have broadened the program to involve parents, the communications media, and the community in promoting norms against drug abuse.

—From *Communities That Care*
HAWKINS, CATALANO AND ASSOCIATES, 1992

Epilogue

~

Recovering alcoholics and addicts sound a deep note of grace in the world. They teach us to value each day for itself, to breathe deeply, and practice simplicity. They show us that redemption from past mistakes is possible—that, however broken our lives, God can restore "the years the locusts have eaten" (Joel 2:25). Even when we have wasted our gifts and talents for years in the pursuit of meaningless goals, and even when we have burdened ourselves with resentments and bitterness, we can still find our way to a transformed, productive life. We can start all over again in partnership with the Divine Light that fills the world.

"It has seemed to me sometimes as though the Lord breathes on this poor gray ember of Creation and it turns to radiance—for a moment or a year or the span of a life," wrote Marilynne Robinson in the book *Gilead*, for which she won the Pulitzer prize:

> And then it sinks back into itself again, and to look at it no one would know it had anything to do with fire, or light.
>
> That is what I said in the Pentecost sermon. I have reflected on that sermon, and there is some truth in it. But the Lord is

more constant and far more extravagant than it seems to imply. Wherever you turn your eyes the world can shine like transfiguration. You don't have to bring a thing to it except a little willingness to see. Only, who could have the courage to see it?[1]

We can have this courage. In joy and gratitude, we can celebrate the many ways in which grace fills the world. We can help bring its transforming power not just to our families and friends, but to our neighbors, our communities, and our world.

ANDERSON SPICKARD JR., MD
BARBARA R. THOMPSON

Appendix A
Letter to Grandchildren

~

Vanderbilt University Medical Center
Nashville, TN

PERSONAL AND CONFIDENTIAL

Robin Smith
Vanderbilt University
Nashville, Tennessee

Dear Robin,

At the request of your grandfather, I am writing you as his physician and a close personal friend. All of the grandchildren of college age in your family will be receiving this letter, and I would appreciate hearing your thoughts on this matter.

As you know, your grandfather is recovering from alcoholism. He is doing extremely well, and we are all grateful that he has received treatment and is maintaining an active role in Alcoholics Anonymous.

You may well be asking, "What does this have to do with me?"

I want to alert you to the fact that heredity plays a strong role in the development of alcoholism. It is thought that the majority of our nation's 18 million alcoholics come from families with an inherited susceptibility to addiction, and numerous studies confirm that alcoholism has a pronounced genetic component.

The evidence in your family is equally striking. Joseph Smith, born in 1881 and the brother of your great-grandfather, was an alcoholic. Mary Doe, your aunt, was also an alcoholic. And of course your grandfather is now recovering from the same disorder.

Perhaps you are wondering what we mean by "alcoholic." Here it is important to distinguish between alcohol *abuse* and alcohol *addiction*. The alcohol abuser frequently drinks to intoxication and may suffer painful consequences from her excessive consumption. However, she can still choose when she drinks, how much she drinks, and if she drinks. The alcohol addict, on the other hand, is no longer in control of her own will, and she cannot predict when or how much she will drink. She continues to drink even after alcohol is causing her serious problems with family, health, jobs, and finances, and she begins to organize her entire life around her need for a drink.

Some of the symptoms of alcohol addiction include guilt and shame about drinking, increased anxiety, relationship problems, blackouts (periods of time when the drinker functions normally but later does not remember what he did), increasing consumption, preoccupation with drinking, and extreme mood swings.

I am writing this letter to inform you that, like your brothers, sisters, and cousins, you may have an inherited tendency toward addiction. Drinking alcoholic beverages is likely to be hazardous to your health, and repeated heavy drinking may lead you unawares into alcoholism. I trust that you will take this warning seriously and that you will make an appropriate decision regarding your own drinking habits. If you have any questions or would like further information, please feel free to write or call.

We love you very much and desire for you a happy, productive life. You come from a distinguished family, and I am certain that you will make a unique contribution with your life. I look forward to meeting you one day.

Sincerely,

ANDERSON SPICKARD JR., MD
Professor of Medicine

Appendix B
MAST: A Diagnostic Test

~

MICHIGAN ALCOHOLISM SCREENING TEST[1]
(MAST) Circle any YES answer.

1. Do you feel you are a normal drinker? (Normal means you drink less than or as much as other people and you have not developed recurring trouble while drinking.)

2. Have you ever awakened the morning after some drinking the night before and found that you could not remember part of the evening?

3. Do either you, your parents, any other near relative, your spouse, or any girlfriend or boyfriend ever worry or complain about your drinking?

4. Can you stop drinking without a struggle after one or two drinks?

5. Do you feel guilty about your drinking?

6. Do friends or relatives think you are a normal drinker?

7. Are you able to stop drinking when you want to?

8. Have you ever attended a meeting of Alcoholics Anonymous (AA)?

9. Have you been in physical fights when you have been drinking?

10. Has your drinking ever created problems between you and either of your parents, another relative, your spouse, or any girlfriend or boyfriend?

11. Has any family member of yours ever gone to anyone for help about your drinking?

12. Have you ever lost friends because of drinking?

13. Have you ever been in trouble at work or at school because of drinking?

14. Have you ever lost a job because of drinking?

15. Have you ever neglected your obligations, your school work, your family, or your job for two or more days in a row because you were drinking?

16. Do you drink before noon fairly often?

17. Have you ever been told you have liver trouble or cirrhosis?

18. After heavy drinking, have you ever had severe shaking, or heard voices or seen things that were not really there?

19. Have you ever gone to anyone for help about your drinking?

20. Have you ever been in a hospital because of drinking?

21. Have you ever been a patient in a psychiatric hospital or on a psychiatric ward of a general hospital where

drinking was part of the problem that resulted in hospitalization?

22. Have you ever been seen at a psychiatric or mental health clinic or gone to any doctor, social worker, or clergy for help with any emotional problem, where drinking was part of the problem?

23. Have you ever been arrested for drunk driving, driving while intoxicated, or driving under the influence of alcoholic beverages or any other drug? (If yes, how many times? _____)

24. Have you ever been arrested or taken into custody, even for a few hours, because of drunken behavior?

KEY TO THE MAST TEST
ANSWERS FOR EACH QUESTION SCORE POINTS IN THE FOLLOWING FASHION:

1. 2 for No
2. 2 for Yes
3. 1 for Yes
4. 2 for No
5. 1 for Yes
6. 2 for No
7. 2 for No
8. 5 for Yes
9. 1 for Yes
10. 2 for Yes
11. 2 for Yes
12. 2 for Yes

13. 2 for Yes

14. 2 for Yes

15. 2 for Yes

16. 1 for Yes

17. 2 for Yes

18. 2 for Yes

19. 5 for Yes

20. 5 for Yes

21. 2 for Yes

22. 2 for Yes

23. 2 for Yes

24. 2 for Yes

1 Score 5 points for hallucinations or delirium tremens
2 Score 2 points for each occasion

INTERPRETATION:

0–3 points = probable normal drinker; 4 points = borderline score; 5–9 points 80% associated with alcoholism/chemical dependence; 10 or more = 100% associated with alcoholism.

Note: As a treating physician, I use the MAST score as a guide to determine the severity of the patient's alcohol dependency. If the score is 10–15, I am comfortable with recommending the patient attend Alcoholics Anonymous meetings regularly. If the score is higher, in the range of 15–20 or above, it is unlikely that AA meetings are enough for the patient, and I recommend inpatient or intensive outpatient treatment after he or she is detoxified.

ANDERSON SPICKARD JR., MD

Appendix C
Resources

WEB SITES

- Cybersober.com: www.cybersober.com. Using the technology of MapQuest, this site generates maps and driving instructions to 133,000 Alcoholics Anonymous, Al-Anon, and other 12-step groups. Other recovery-related information and online meetings are available. A membership fee is required for use of services.

- Christians in Recovery: www.christians-in-recovery.com

- Hazelden Foundation: www.hazelden.org

- The Intervention Resource Center: www.interventioninfo.org

- Jewish Alcoholics, Chemically Dependent Persons, and Significant Others: www.jacsweb.org

- National Association for Children of Alcoholics: www.nacoa.org

- National Council on Alcoholism and Other Drug Dependence: www.ncadd.org

- National Institute on Alcohol Abuse and Alcoholism: www.niaaa.nih.gov

- Sober.com: a listing of all treatment centers by state and county in the U.S.: www.sober.com

- U.S. Drug Rehab Center: a listing of 14,000 drug and alcohol treatment centers: www.usdrugrehabcenters.com

BOOKS AND PUBLICATIONS

- Stephanie Brown and Virginia Lewis, *The Alcoholic Family in Recovery: A Developmental Model* (New York: Guilford Press, 1999). Designed for therapists and families alike, a comprehensive guide to long-term family recovery.

- Sharon Wegsheider-Cruse, *Another Chance: Hope and Health for the Alcoholic Family* (Palo Alto, CA: Science and Behavior Books, 1989). A classic text about family roles and the dynamics of addiction.

- Jeff Jay and Debra Jay, *Love First: A New Approach to Intervention for Alcoholism and Drug Addiction* (Center City, MN: Hazelden, 2000). A step-by-step self-help book about intervention.

- Bessel A. van der Kolk, Alexander C. McFarlane, and Lars Weisaeth, eds., *Traumatic Stress: The Effects of Overwhelming Experience on Mind, Body, and Society* (New York: Guilford Press, 1996). A comprehensive and readable book covering all aspects of trauma and recovery for doctors and substance abuse professionals.

- William R. Miller and Stephen Rollnick, *Motivational Interviewing: Preparing People for Change* (New York:

Guilford Press, 2002). A groundbreaking book on "motivational interviewing," and a research-based approach to helping patients find the motivation to enter treatment and maintain sobriety.

- George E. Vaillant, *The Natural History of Alcoholism Revisited* (Cambridge, MA: Harvard University Press, 1995). Based on a sixty-year study at Harvard University, this book is an outstanding reference book for doctors and other substance abuse professionals.

- Robert K. White and Deborah George Wright, *Addiction Intervention: Strategies to Motivate Treatment-Seeking Behavior* (Binghamton, NY: Haworth Press, 1998). This book contains strategies to help motivate addicts to seek treatment.

12-STEP ORGANIZATIONS

- Al-Anon/Alateen Family Group, (888) 4AL-ANON. Web site: www.al-anon.org. A self-help organization to help family and friends deal with an alcoholic loved one. Alateen is a similar program for youth.

- Alcoholics Anonymous, (212) 870-3400. Web site: www.alcoholics-anonymous.org. A fellowship of men and women who have a drinking problem. Meetings are held daily all over the world, are free, and open to anyone with a drinking problem.

ALCOHOL AND DRUG TREATMENT CENTERS

- Cumberland Heights, www.cumberlandheights.org. Located on the banks of the Cumberland River near Nashville, Tennessee. Outpatient and residential programs are for adults and young people with alcohol and drug dependency.

- Hazelden, www.hazelden.org; (800) 257.7810. Mailing address: CO3, PO Box 11, Center City, MN 55012-0111. Founded in 1949, Hazelden is an internationally recognized pioneer in the field of drug and alcohol treatment and education, with residential treatment centers in several states.

- Sante Center for Healing, www.santecenter.com; (800) 258-4250. An adult (18 and up) poly-addiction residential treatment center located in Argyle, Texas.

- Talbott Recovery Campus, www.talbottcampus.com; (800) 445-4232. A residential treatment center in Atlanta, Georgia, for persons with alcohol and other drug dependencies.

HELP AND INFORMATION

- Hazelden, www.hazelden.org; (800) 257-7810. Education, information, screening and assessment.

- National Institute on Alcohol Abuse and Alcoholism (NIAAA), www.niaaa.nih.gov. Comprehensive education and resource site, with answers to frequently asked questions.

- SAMHSA National Clearinghouse for Alcohol and Drug Information, www.health.org; (800) 729-6686. For free publications on alcohol and drug abuse, 24 hours a day, seven days a week.

Notes

⤙

Chapter 1

1. Barbara R. Thompson, "Global Binge," *World Vision* (December 1996/January 1997), 2–5.

Chapter 2

1. A word of caution: This test can be self-administered, but please note its reliability depends on following the exact wording of the questions. Also, a screening test alone does not provide enough information to make a diagnosis, and it is important to consult a physician or other professional with a specialty in substance abuse for a diagnosis and a treatment plan. A longer, more elaborate diagnostic tool, the Michigan Alcoholism Screening Test (MAST), is reproduced in Appendix B.

2. J. A. Ewing, "Detecting Alcoholism: The CAGE Questionnaire," *Journal of the American Medical Association* (1984): 1905–07.

Chapter 3

1. George E. Vaillant, *The Natural History of Alcoholism Revisited* (Cambridge, MA: Harvard University Press, 1995), 75ff.

2. Ibid., 381.

3. In the 1970s and 1980s, separate studies by D. W. Goodwin and R. J. Cadoret and their colleagues demonstrated that, in the absence of a family inheritance pattern, adopted children raised in alcoholic homes, are not at increased risk for addiction:

D. W. Goodwin, F. Schulsinger, N. Moller, L. Hermansen, G. Winokur, S. B. Guze, "Drinking problems in adopted and nonadopted sons of alcoholics," *Archives of General Psychiatry,* 1974, 31: 164–69.

R. J. Cadoret, C. A. Cain, W. M. Grove, "Development of alcoholism in adoptees raised apart from alcoholic biologic relatives," *Archives of General Psychiatry,* 1980, 37: 561–63.

4. Glenn D. Walters, "The heritability of alcohol abuse and dependence: a meta-analysis of behavior genetic research," *American Journal of Drug and Alcohol Abuse* (August 2002): 1.

5. Proceedings published in *Alcoholism: Clinical & Experimental Research,* February 2005, quoted in "Teen Brain: 'A Work in Progress,'" http://alcoholism.about.com/of/teens/a/blacer050216.htm (June 2005).

6. Jane J. Stein, ed., "Substance Abuse: The Nation's Number One Health Problem," *The Robert Wood Johnson Foundation Key Indicators for Policy, 2001* (Princeton, NJ: 2001), 30.

7. Bessel A. van der Kolk, Alexander C. McFarlane, and Lars Weisaeth, eds., *Traumatic Stress: The Effects of Overwhelming Experience on Mind, Body, and Society* (New York: Guilford Press, 1996), 5.

8. Calvin Trillin, "U.S. Journal: Gallup, New Mexico," *The New Yorker,* 25 September 1971, 108.

9. Stein, "Substance Abuse," 18.

10. Vaillant, *The Natural History,* 59ff.

CHAPTER 4

1. Marty Mann, *New Primer on Alcoholism* (New York: Holt, Rinehart, and Winston, 1968), 27.

CHAPTER 5

1. As quoted in Andrew Sorenson, *Alcoholic Priests* (New York: Seabury Press, 1976), 158.

2. Peter R. Martin et al, eds., "Alcohol and Other Abused Substances," in *Principles of Pharmacology: Basic Concepts and Clinical Applications* (New York: Chapman & Hall, 1995), 423.

3. Eric J. Nestler and Robert C. Malenka, "The Addicted Brain," *ScientificAmerican.com,* 9 February 2004, 1.

4. Peter R. Martin and Dieter Meyerhoff, *Alcoholism: Clinical and Experimental Research*, April 2004, 28(4): 650–61.
5. *Brown University DATA*, vol. 15, no. 3, March 1996.
6. Stein, "Substance Abuse," 17.

CHAPTER 6

1. The National Mental Health Association estimates that substance abuse may account for more than half of all suicides.
2. Vernon E. Johnson, *I'll Quit Tomorrow* (San Francisco: Harper and Row, 1980), 39.

CHAPTER 8

1. Johnson, *I'll Quit Tomorrow*, 41.
2. When we first published *Dying for a Drink*, only 3 percent of medical students had substance abuse training; today that number has risen to almost 80 percent.
3. Mark Bloom, "Impaired Physicians: Medicine Bites the Bullet," *Medical World News*, 24 July 1978, 41.

CHAPTER 10

1. John Boit Morse, *Don't Tell Me I'm Not an Alcoholic* (pamphlet), (Center City, MN: Hazelden Foundation), 4.
2. Joseph Kellerman, *A Guide for the Family of the Alcoholic* (pamphlet), (Charlotte, NC: Charlotte Council on Alcoholism Groups), 7.

CHAPTER 11

1. Stephanie Lewis Harter and Tracey L. Taylor, *Journal of Substance Abuse* (2000): vol. 11, no. 1, 31–44.

CHAPTER 12

1. Stein, "Substance Abuse," 60.
2. Ibid., 62.
3. *A Letter to Our Alcoholic Dad* (pamphlet), (Center City, MN: Hazelden Foundation, 1977).

CHAPTER 13

1. Claudia Black and Sharon Wegsheider have identified and explored these roles more fully in their landmark books, respectively, *It Will Never Happen to Me* (New York: Balantine Books, 1991) and

Another Chance: Hope and Health for the Alcoholic Family (Palo Alto, CA: Science & Behavior Books, 1981). These books have become classics in the field and are resources for professionals as well as children of alcoholics of all ages.

2. Robert F. Anda, et al. "Adverse Childhood Experiences, Alcoholic Parents, and Later Risk of Alcoholism and Depression," Psychiatric Services, http://psychservices.psychiatryonline.org, August 2002, vol. 53. no. 8. Referencing Cotton NS, "The familial incidence of alcoholism: a review." *Journal of Studies on Alcohol* (1979): 40:89–116.

3. Ibid.

CHAPTER 14

1. Stein, "Substance Abuse," 104–6.

2. There are notable exceptions to this rule. Almost everyone has heard of a now solid citizen who has recovered from a skid-row existence, and it is important not to rule out hope for any addicted drinker. At the same time, the drama of these stories lies in the fact that such recoveries are the exception, not the rule.

CHAPTER 15

1. *Alcoholics Anonymous* (New York: Alcoholics Anonymous World Services, Inc., 1976), xxvi.

2. William R. Miller, Robert J. Meyers, and J. Scott Tonigan, "Engaging the Unmotivated in Treatment for Alcohol Problems: A Comparison of Three Strategies for Intervention Through Family Members," *Journal of Consulting and Clinical Psychology* (1999): vol. 67, no. 5, 688–97.

CHAPTER 16

1. William R. Miller and Stephen Rollnick, *Motivational Interviewing: Preparing People for Change* (New York: Guilford Press, 2002), 17–18.

CHAPTER 17

1. Michael Fleming and Linda Baier Manwell, "Brief Intervention in Primary Care Settings," *Alcohol Research & Health* (1999): vol. 23, no. 2.

Notes

2. AA's twelfth step reads, "Having had a spiritual awakening as a result of these steps, we try to carry this message to alcoholics and practice these principles in all our affairs."
3. Motivational interviewing combines the client-centered therapy of Carl Rogers with the research of J. O. Prochaska into the stages of change. Prochaska identified five stages of change: pre-contemplation, contemplation, preparation, taking action, and maintenance.
4. Miller and Rollnick, *Motivational Interviewing.*
5. Miller, Meyers, and Tonigan, "Engaging the Unmotivated in Treatment for Alcohol Problems," 688–97.

CHAPTER 18
1. For more information on talking with children about family alcoholism, contact the National Association for Children of Alcoholics at www.health.org/nacoa/.

CHAPTER 19
1. Jeff and Debra Jay, *Love First* (Center City, MN: Hazelden, 2000), 48–49.

CHAPTER 20
1. For more about DT's, see Chapter 6.

CHAPTER 21
1. Vaillant, *The Natural History of Alcoholism Revisited,* 254.
2. This includes prescribing Antabuse to reduce the chance of drinking again, or naltrexone or acamprosate to diminish the power of addictive craving. It also includes monitoring the prescription drug use of individuals with a coexisting mental illness.
3. *Alcoholics Anonymous,* 58.
4. "The Twelve Steps" and a brief excerpt from the text, *Alcoholics Anonymous,* are reprinted with permission of Alcoholics Anonymous World Services, Inc. (A.A.W.S.). Permission to reprint the Twelve Steps and a brief excerpt does not mean that A.A.W.S. has reviewed or approved the contents of this publication or that A.A.W.S. necessarily agrees with the views expressed therein. AA is a program of recovery from alcoholism *only*—use of

the Twelve Steps in connection with programs and activities that are patterned after AA but address other problems, or in any other non-AA context, does not imply otherwise.

CHAPTER 23

1. Andre Corley, "Triggers: What Are They and Why They Are Important," *Sante News*, Argyle, Texas, undated.
2. *Alcoholics Anonymous*, 66.
3. Ibid., 64–68.
4. Antabuse is not a cure for addiction, but it can be helpful in conjunction with treatment. Some alcoholics take a half pill daily for their entire life as an extra safeguard against an impulsive drink. Antabuse is effective for up to four or five days after ingestion and allows the alcoholic time to get a hold on her craving. Persons taking Antabuse must be careful to avoid all medications containing alcohol; the risks of mixing alcohol and Antabuse include serious convulsions and death.

CHAPTER 25

1. Nestler and Malenka, "The Addicted Brain," 1.

CHAPTER 27

1. Earl W. Foell, "The Beethoven's 9th in Asia Effect," *The Christian Science Monitor*, 90th Anniversary Edition, 25 November 1998.
2. Morton Mintz, "Alcohol Inc.: Bartender to the World," *The Washington Post*, 4 September 1983, C2.
3. As cited in Margaret A. Fuad, ed., *Alcohol Network News* (February 1983), 4.
4. Mark Noll, "America's Battle Against the Bottle, *Christianity Today*, vol. 23, 17 January 1979, 21.
5. Interestingly, Mikhail Gorbachev's effort to curtail alcohol consumption in the former Soviet Union also resulted in a dramatic decline in alcohol-related problems. But it likewise opened the door for organized crime to take over the alcohol industry.
6. Stephanie Brown and Virginia Lewis, *The Alcoholic Family in Recovery: A Developmental Model* (New York: Guilford Press, 1999), 35.
7. This enhanced risk may also come from a family history of alco-

holism. Dogmatic teetotalers may take their stand as a result of their personal and painful experience of living with an alcoholic.

8. Willmar Thorkelson, "Alcoholism," *A.D.* (January 1982), 12.

9. Ruth C. Engs, "Drinking Patterns and Attitudes Toward Alcoholism of Australian Human Service Students," *Journal of Studies on Alcohol,* vol. 43, no. 5 (1982): 528.

10. Samuel M. Shoemaker, "The Spiritual Angle," *The Grapevine* (October 1955), 17–18.

11. Vaillant, *The Natural History of Alcoholism Revisited,* 243.

EPILOGUE

1. Marilynne Robinson, *Gilead* (New York: Farrar, Straus and Giroux, 2004), 245.

APPENDIX B

1. M. L. Selzer, "The Michigan Alcoholism Screening Test (MAST): The quest for a new diagnostic instrument," *American Journal of Psychiatry* (1971): 127, 1653–58.

About the Authors

~

ANDERSON SPICKARD JR., is a professor of medicine and psychiatry at Vanderbilt University Medical Center, where he holds the Chancellor's Chair in Medicine and is the medical director of the Center for Professional Health.

BARBARA R. THOMPSON is an award-winning author specializing in social and international issues. She wrote and co-produced *Innocents: The Trials and Triumphs of Children of War,* which captures the stories and photographs of children growing up in violent circumstances around the world. Ms. Thompson is the co-founder of International Community School, a school for refugee and mainstream children in Atlanta, Georgia.